Accounting for Success

Making sense of Solicitors' Accounts for LPC students, practitioners and law firm cashiers

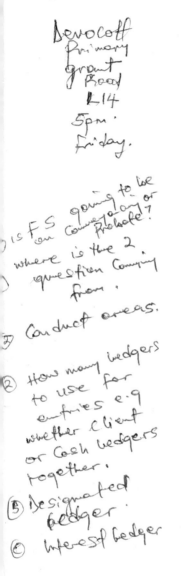

Devocoff
Primary
Grant
Road
L14
5pm.
Friday.

1) is FS going to be on conveyancing or Probate?
where is the 2. question coming from.

3) Conduct areas.

2) How many ledgers to use for entries e.g. whether Client or Cash ledgers together.

5) Designated ledger.

6) Interest ledger

Accounting for Success

Making sense of Solicitors' Accounts for LPC students,
practitioners and law firm cashiers

Third edition

Roy Chandler BSc (Econ), FCA
Professor in Accounting, Cardiff Business School

John Loosemore BA, Solicitor
Managing Director, Altior Consulting & Training
Formerly Senior Lecturer in Law, University of Wales, College of Cardiff

Butterworths
LexisNexis™

Members of the LexisNexis Group worldwide

United Kingdom	Butterworths Tolley, a Division of Reed Elsevier (UK) Ltd, Halsbury House, 35 Chancery Lane, LONDON, WC2A 1EL, and 4 Hill Street, EDINBURGH EH2 3JZ
Argentina	Abeledo Perrot, Jurisprudencia Argentina and Depalma, BUENOS AIRES
Australia	Butterworths, a Division of Reed International Books Australia Pty Ltd, CHATSWOOD, New South Wales
Austria	ARD Betriebsdienst and Verlag Orac, VIENNA
Canada	Butterworths Canada Ltd, MARKHAM, Ontario
Chile	Publitecsa and Conosur Ltda, SANTIAGO DE CHILE
Czech Republic	Orac sro, PRAGUE
France	Editions du Juris-Classeur SA, PARIS
Hong Kong	Butterworths Asia (Hong Kong), HONG KONG
Hungary	Hvg Orac, BUDAPEST
India	Butterworths India, NEW DELHI
Ireland	Butterworths (Ireland) Ltd, DUBLIN
Italy	Giuffré, MILAN
Malaysia	Malayan Law Journal Sdn Bhd, KUALA LUMPUR
New Zealand	Butterworths of New Zealand, WELLINGTON
Poland	Wydawnictwa Prawnicze PWN, WARSAW
Singapore	Butterworths Asia, SINGAPORE
South Africa	Butterworths Publishers (Pty) Ltd, DURBAN
Switzerland	Stämpfli Verlag AG, BERNE
USA	LexisNexis, DAYTON, Ohio

A CIP Catalogue record for this book is available from the British Library.

ISBN 0 406 95299 X

Typeset by Doyle & Co, Colchester
Printed and bound in Great Britain by William Clowes Limited, Beccles, London

Visit Butterworths LexisNexis *direct* at www.butterworths.com

Preface

We are delighted that demand for this book has been such that sales have again exhausted the print run within three years, thus necessitating a new edition. We have taken this opportunity to update the text to incorporate developments since the last edition and to make further revisions in the light of our experience in using that edition as a teaching aid. We are also grateful to those readers who made helpful and constructive comments on the two previous editions.

The book has been written specifically for both practitioners and students of law. The material in the text reflects our extensive practical and teaching experience. The exercises and worked examples in the text have been tested and refined in face-to-face tuition over several years.

We must emphasise again that accounting is an essential discipline in business and commerce; in fact, accounting has been described as the language of business and, as with any language, practice comes before mastery. Therefore, we believe that it is essential that readers diligently attempt to answer the exercises in the text and, if necessary, re-work them.

We have found that one of the first difficulties in understanding accounting is the use of everyday expressions in particular ways which are not always intuitively obvious. The very term 'accounts' is used in numerous ways in practice. 'Accounts' can refer to banking accounts, individual ledger accounts or even the underlying, basic accounting records – the Solicitors' Accounts Rules (SAR) are themselves guilty of this ambiguity. 'Accounts' may also be used in relation to the financial statements of legal practices or other organisations. Although this text covers all these uses, we aim to make our particular meaning clear whenever we use the term 'accounts'.

To help clarify an understanding of accounting, we have included a glossary with brief explanations of the most common terms. Again, diligent application to the study of accounting will bring a familiarity with these terms and with techniques which will quickly clarify any early confusion.

Another obstacle to the successful pursuit of studying of accounting is overcoming the fear of numbers. Lawyers, used to coping with words, often freeze at the thought of handling numbers. This is not a new problem, as is evidenced by a quotation from nearly 100 years ago:

> 'The work of figures is in its nature a speciality, proficiency in which is not too frequently found in conjunction with the legal mind proper.' ((1904) 16 Juridical Review at 426).

There is a common conception that accounting requires great mathematical ability. This is entirely untrue. In most cases all that is required is a knowledge of basic arithmetical concepts such as addition and subtraction! Confidence in dealing with numbers and numerical concepts will come with practice.

This brings us to the final obstacle, indifference. Lawyers may fail to see the need to study accounting because they know that, in practice, many law firms employ in-house book-keepers or accountants and have computerised systems. This attitude overlooks the fact that though the maintaining of accounting records may be delegated to book-keepers, responsibility for compliance with the Law Society's rules remains with the solicitor. The buck cannot be passed to employees. Failure to comply with the SAR is one of the most common causes of disciplinary action against solicitors, and can carry heavy financial and other penalties. Equally important, an understanding of accounts is essential for the delivery of a quality legal service to clients and for the successful management of law firms.

LPC Students

This is an ideal text for the Accounts Syllabus of the Legal Practice Course.

Use by law firms

The text will be helpful to practitioners whose education and training is in need of updating or who wish to use it for in-house training. The need for professionals to acquire basic financial skills is becoming increasingly important in all walks of life. In the legal profession, financial skills are needed not only in advising clients, but also in managing the practice. Firms will run into financial difficulties if partners neglect the management of the firm's finances.

Tutor Manual

A Tutor Manual is also available for those who adopt the text for their courses and in-house training. The *Manual* contains solutions to the exercises in the text with commentary on points arising from the exercises and the text itself. The *Manual* can be obtained from The Publisher, Academic Publishing, Butterworths, 35 Chancery Lane, London, WC2A 1EL.

Updating

The text is based on the SAR 1998 as set out in Chapter 28 of the Law Society's *Guide to Professional Conduct of Solicitors* (8th edn). As with the study of any professional topic, the need to keep up to date is of paramount importance; the reader should be aware that the rules and the Society's guidance on their application are subject to change and should refer to the *Law Society Gazette* and the Society's web-site: www.lawsociety.org.uk.

Roy Chandler
John Loosemore
Cardiff

March 2002

Contents

Glossary of accounting terms

ACCRUALS

Expenses incurred in one period but not paid for during that period.

ACCUMULATED DEPRECIATION

The amount of depreciation charged over the expired life of a fixed asset, also known as 'the provision for depreciation'.

ASSETS

Resources yielding future economic benefit owned by a business. Current assets are those which will be realised (or create benefits) within the next accounting period; fixed or long-term assets may provide benefits over a longer term.

BAD DEBTS

Debts owed to a business which are irrecoverable.

BALANCE SHEET

Reflects the financial position of a business at one point in time.

BOOK VALUE

The value for assets at cost, less accumulated depreciation, also referred to as 'net book value'.

CAPITAL

The owners' investment in the business, equivalent to the assets less liabilities.

CAPITAL EXPENDITURE

Expenditure which has been capitalised, ie treated as a long-term asset rather than written off as an expense against profit.

CASH FLOW STATEMENT

Summary of cash movements during the year.

CONSOLIDATED ACCOUNTS

Accounts prepared for a group of companies as if it were a single company.

CREDITORS

Persons to whom the business owes money.

CURRENT ACCOUNT
Used mainly in partnerships to record the amount owed to or by a partner, the balance is usually the partner's share of profits less any drawings.

CURRENT ASSETS
Assets normally consumed or turned into cash within the next period.

CURRENT LIABILITIES
Claims on the assets expected to be settled in the next accounting period.

DEBENTURES
A form of long-term loan to the business.

DEBTORS
Persons who owe money to the business.

DEPRECIATION
The amount of the original cost of a fixed asset charged against the profit of one accounting period, in an attempt to spread the cost over the expected useful life.

DRAWINGS
Cash or goods withdrawn by the owner from the business for private use or consumption.

EQUITY
The owners' investment in the business, usually original capital and retained profit (also called 'capital').

FIXED ASSETS
Assets having an expected useful life in excess of one year.

GEARING
Long-term debt expressed as a proportion of total long term finance (long-term debt and equity).

GROSS PROFIT
Measured by deducting cost of sales from sales. It is a measure of the profit margin, ie difference between buying and selling prices before overhead expenses are taken into account.

HISTORICAL COST
An accounting convention whereby assets are recorded at original cost (less amounts written off) with no attempt to reflect current market value.

LIABILITIES
These reflect future claims on the assets of the business. Current liabilities are those which will have to be paid in the next accounting period. Long-term liabilities are those whose repayment date is more than one year after the balance sheet date.

NET ASSETS
Assets less liabilities.

NET CURRENT ASSETS
Current assets less current liabilities where the former exceed the latter.

NET CURRENT LIABILITIES
Current assets less current liabilities where the latter exceed the former.

NET PROFIT	Income less all expenses.
PREPAYMENTS	Expenditure which relates to a future period.
PROFIT AND LOSS ACCOUNT	An accounting statement showing the profit or loss resulting from a period's transactions.
PROVISIONS	Amounts written off to reflect the loss in 'value' of an asset.
RESERVES/RETAINED PROFITS	Profits made but retained in the business, ie not paid to owners by drawings or dividends.
STOCK	Goods bought for resale remaining unsold at the end of a period.
TURNOVER	Another term for sales.
WORK-IN-PROGRESS	The cost of partly finished goods or, in the case of professional practices, incomplete work not yet billed.

Chapter 1

Introduction to basic book-keeping

INTRODUCTION

'The uninitiated are filled with a sort of mysterious terror when brought face to face with a simple question in accounting . . . Gentlemen of the legal profession are by no means exempt from it.' (Muir *The Accountant* 30 January 1892, p 103)

'The inability of lawyers to grasp anything more complicated than a Cash Account is proverbial.' (*The Accountant* 10 November 1894, p 982)

The above quotations have lost none of their relevance despite the passing of more than a century. They show that, for some reason, lawyers have always struggled to come to terms with accounting. Our intention is to provide a textbook which will enable the ordinary lawyer to grasp the mysteries of accounting.

THE HISTORICAL BACKGROUND

Historians have been able to trace accounting records from the earliest civilisations, showing that, from a very early point in history, the need for proper accounting was recognised. In most cases the surviving accounting records deal with the accountability of public money, reflecting the need to demonstrate that tax contributions had been properly accounted for. The forms of records used and the methods employed to check their accuracy have changed over the centuries, but the fundamental concept of accountability remains unchanged to this day. Those who have custody over other people's money must not only keep adequate records to show what has happened to that money but also be prepared to subject themselves and their records to some form of check. This concept is evident in the Solicitors' Accounts Rules 1998 (hereafter the SAR).

THE NEED FOR ACCOUNTS

Accounting now serves many purposes. Its primary role is to provide a way of demonstrating that stewards (the agents) have taken proper care over the owners' (the principals') assets. An everyday example of the rendering of an account is the requirement for banks to provide customers with regular bank statements – the banks are agents who are accountable to their customers. Similarly, company directors are required to present annual accounts to shareholders. The fact that company accounts have to be filed as public documents indicates that present accountability relationships extend beyond the shareholders. Other parties have a legitimate interest in and a right to information from companies; for example, creditors, lenders, customers, employees, tax authorities and other government departments.

Accounting information is also essential for the efficient running of any business, including a legal practice. Without accurate information on the financial affairs of the practice, the partners will not be able to plan for future development.

THE DOUBLE-ENTRY PRINCIPLE

The principle of double-entry book-keeping was first documented over 500 years ago in Italy, where it was used by merchants and traders to record and control their business affairs. Despite the enormous advances in information technology and computerised systems, double-entry remains the basis of accounting today. The SAR do not specifically refer to the double-entry principle, although it is implicit in r 32(2-4). However, the Law Society Guidelines 'Accounting Procedures and Systems' (SAR, Appendix 3) are more specific. Paragraph 2.3 states that: 'Proper books of account should be maintained on the double-entry principle.'

WHAT IS DOUBLE-ENTRY BOOK-KEEPING?

The double-entry principle recognises and reflects the fact that every transaction has two effects. This is true of both personal and commercial transactions. For example, the purchase of this book was a single transaction but it had two effects: each purchaser's bank balance decreased (or their credit card liability increased) and their stock of books increased.

The basic accounting record of transactions is a ledger account. Each type of transaction is recorded in a separate ledger account. Each ledger account has two columns for recording the monetary amounts of each transaction, the debits and credits. The column headings of DR and CR are evidence of the enduring legacy of the Italian origins of this book-keeping system (debitor and creditor were the original terms).

A LEDGER ACCOUNT				
Date	Detail	DR	CR	Balance

In this respect a ledger account resembles a familiar bank statement. Unfortunately, the familiarity is also the cause of the initial confusion over the terms 'debits' and 'credits', as will be illustrated in the following examples.

EXAMPLE

Suppose Samantha is a law student who starts the LPC in September having just opened a bank account with a cheque for £1,000 for work on a research project during her summer vacation. On 3 September, she buys groceries for £50 by cheque. She uses her bank account debit card to buy books from Millstones for £60 on 15 September. On 23 September she buys by cheque more groceries for £50 and sends a cheque for £150 rent to her landlord. Assuming no other transactions occur, her bank statement will appear as follows:

BANK STATEMENT				
Date	Detail	Payments (Debits)	Receipts (Credits)	Balance
Sept 1	Deposit		1,000.00	1,000.00 CR
Sept 3	Cheque 000001	50.00		950.00 CR
Sept 15	Millstones debitcard	60.00		890.00 CR
Sept 23	Cheque 000002	50.00		840.00 CR
	Cheque 000003	150.00		690.00 CR

Notes

1. It is important to appreciate that the bank statement is a copy of the bank's ledger account for this particular customer.
2. The date column is necessary to provide an 'audit trail' for the bank's own purposes and to provide the customer with a useful check on the statement's accuracy, though the date is not repeated for transactions occurring on the same day.
3. The detail column briefly describes the method of payment or receipt and the recipient or source of the money.
4. The balance column provides an 'at-a-glance' check on the current position, which is useful to both banker and client.
5. The relevance to solicitors of the above points will become clearer later.

Some people keep no records of their own income and expenditure, relying entirely on the bank to provide them with information. More cautious people keep an informal record of receipts, payments and bank balance in a notebook or on their chequebook stubs. Few people keep full double-entry records in ledger accounts for their personal transactions, *but* all businesses of any significant size should keep such accounts.

At this early stage we need to clear up the confusion over 'debits' and 'credits' which arises because students often approach the subject of accounting from the same standpoint as they view the bank statement entries.

CONFUSION OVER DEBITS AND CREDITS

The words 'debits' and 'credits' often cause confusion because, in everyday life, the most familiar use of the terms is on bank statements; your bank account is *credited* with cash which you pay in and it is *debited* with items which you pay out, by cash withdrawal, cheque, standing order or direct debit. In the ledger account for the cash of a business, debits and credits are used the other way around. The ledger account recording the movements and balance of cash is *debited* with money paid *in* and *credited* with money paid *out*. The explanation for the way the banks use the terms is that they are looking at transactions from their own book-keeping perspective: when you pay money into your bank account you become a creditor of the bank, they owe you that money. When you withdraw money from the account or make a payment from it, the bank's debt to you is reduced.

If you were to keep double-entry accounts, your ledger account recording the money in your bank account (we call this your 'cash account') would be the mirror image of the bank statement: a credit on the bank statement will be a debit in your own cash account and a debit on the bank statement will be a credit in your cash account.

Let us now set up the double-entry records for Samantha. There will be a separate ledger account for each type or category of transaction. By convention the debit entry is made in the account of the item for which a payment is made (ie the benefit received) and the credit entry is entered in the account of the source of the finance for the transaction (ie the item which provides the benefit). Thus, each transaction will result in an entry in two accounts, ie two entries.

EXAMPLE

Samantha received £1,000 on 1 September and paid this into her bank account. If she kept full ledger accounts, she would need a ledger account to keep track of her money (a cash account) and a ledger account for each of her types of income and expenditure. When she banks her pay cheque, her cash position improves – cash receives the benefit, so the cash account is debited with £1,000.

CASH/BANK ACCOUNT				
Date	Detail	DR	CR	Balance
1 Sept	Income	1,000.00		1,000.00 DR

Notes

1. The debit balance indicates that at this stage the bank owes Samantha £1,000; it is in debt due to Samantha.
2. This is consistent with the bank's own ledger account (as reproduced in its bank statement), a credit balance on an individual's statement shows that the individual is a creditor of the bank (the bank owes the customer money).

Under the double-entry system every debit must have an equal and opposite entry, a credit. So we now have to ask where the money came from. The source of the cash was the income from the vacation job and we need to open an account for this item:

INCOME ACCOUNT				
Date	Detail	DR	CR	Balance
1 Sept	Income		1,000.00	1,000.00 CR

Notes

1. The detail column contains a very brief narrative entry which is simply the name of the other account containing the corresponding double-entry. This provides an audit trail and allows the accuracy of the book-keeping to be confirmed at a later date.
2. The credit balance on the income account shows that this is the source of the money.
3. The debit balance on the cash account matches the credit balance on the income account.

The second transaction involves the purchase of groceries and the double-entry is:

CASH/BANK ACCOUNT				
Date	Detail	DR	CR	Balance
1 Sept	Income	1,000.00		1,000.00 DR
3 Sept	Groceries		50.00	950.00 DR

to record the payment, and:

GROCERIES ACCOUNT				
Date	Detail	DR	CR	Balance
3 Sept	Cash	50.00		50.00 DR

to record the acquisition of the groceries. The debit balance explains the purpose for which the money has been spent, ie purchase of groceries.

The third transaction is the purchase of books:

CASH/BANK ACCOUNT				
Date	Detail	DR	CR	Balance
1 Sept	Income	1,000.00		1,000.00 DR
3 Sept	Groceries		50.00	950.00 DR
15 Sept	Books		60.00	890.00 DR

BOOKS ACCOUNT				
Date	Detail	DR	CR	Balance
15 Sept	Cash	60.00		60.00 DR

The fourth and fifth transactions are the purchase of more groceries and the payment of rent, both on 23 September:

CASH/BANK ACCOUNT				
Date	Detail	DR	CR	Balance
1 Sept	Income	1,000.00		1,000.00 DR
3 Sept	Groceries		50.00	950.00 DR
15 Sept	Books		60.00	890.00 DR
23 Sept	Groceries		50.00	
	Rent		150.00	690.00 DR

GROCERIES ACCOUNT				
Date	Detail	DR	CR	Balance
3 Sept	Cash	50.00		50.00 DR
23 Sept	Cash	50.00		100.00 DR

RENT ACCOUNT				
Date	Detail	DR	CR	Balance
23 Sept	Cash	150.00		150.00 DR

Notes

1. The same groceries account is used. Separate accounts are opened for each *type* of transaction, not for each transaction.
2. The running balance on each account provides important information, the cumulative total of expenditure on that particular item.

Now the complete set of records will appear as:

CASH/BANK ACCOUNT				
Date	Detail	DR	CR	Balance
1 Sept	Income	1,000.00		1,000.00 DR
3 Sept	Groceries		50.00	950.00 DR
15 Sept	Books		60.00	890.00 DR
23 Sept	Groceries		50.00	
	Rent		150.00	690.00 DR

INCOME ACCOUNT				
Date	Detail	DR	CR	Balance
1 Sept	Income		1,000.00	1,000.00 CR

GROCERIES ACCOUNT				
Date	Detail	DR	CR	Balance
3 Sept	Cash	50.00		50.00 DR
23 Sept	Cash	50.00		100.00 DR

BOOKS ACCOUNT				
Date	Detail	DR	CR	Balance
15 Sept	Cash	60.00		60.00 DR

RENT ACCOUNT				
Date	Detail	DR	CR	Balance
23 Sept	Cash	150.00		150.00 DR

TRIAL BALANCE

Since every transaction results in two entries, a debit and a credit, the sum of all the debit entries must equal the sum of all the credit entries, provided of course that each transaction has been recorded properly.

When all the transactions have been recorded, a list of all the final debit and credit balances is extracted to prove the arithmetical accuracy of the record-keeping. This statement or list of balances is known as a 'trial balance'. For example, a list of the closing balances from the illustration above would appear as:

TRIAL BALANCE		
	DR	CR
Income		1,000.00
Books	60.00	
Rent	150.00	
Groceries	100.00	
Cash	690.00	
Total	1,000.00	1,000.00

This 'balancing' is a valuable check on the record-keeping. (In fact, it is so important that the SAR require solicitors holding clients' money every month to perform a similar exercise on their records of clients' money.) If the total of the debit balances does not equal the total of the credit balances, we know that a mistake must have been made. Once the trial balance has been extracted and balanced, we can proceed to the preparation of the final accounts, the profit and loss account and the balance sheet. The preparation of these statements will be covered later on.

CONCLUSION

The double-entry system of book-keeping has significant advantages over other systems (such as keeping only a cash book):

1. It provides a complete record of all transactions – the books of account provide answers to any queries raised about any transaction.

2. Since every debit entry is matched with every credit entry, the total of all debit balances should equal the total of all credit balances – hence the system provides an in-built arithmetical check on the accuracy of the recording.

3. The system can be utilised to deter fraud by, for example, allocating responsibility for entering credits to one book-keeper while another is responsible for making debit entries.

The purpose of this chapter was to introduce the basic notion that every transaction has two effects and to show how the double-entry system captures and records both effects. It is essential that the principles of double-entry are understood before we move on to consider particular aspects of accounting by solicitors.

EXERCISES

1. Explain the need for individuals, businesses and other organisations to keep accounts.

2. Who might have a legitimate interest in the accounts of a limited company?

3. Explain the basic principle behind double-entry book-keeping.

4. If accounts are kept on the double-entry principle, explain why the debits and credits in the cash account are the reverse of the debits and credits on a bank statement.

5. Under the double-entry system, what are the two entries to record a payment of £45 for a telephone bill?

6. Under the double-entry system, which account is debited when the monthly salary or other form of income is received?

7. What is the purpose of preparing a trial balance?

Chapter 2

Introduction to solicitors' accounts

INTRODUCTION

Solicitors very often handle money belonging to clients when acting in various types of matters, both contentious and non-contentious. Following a spate of embezzlements by solicitors, including even a former President of the Law Society, the need to keep clients' money not only safe but also separate from the solicitors' own money was accepted by some members of the Law Society before the end of the nineteenth century. However, it was not until more scandals occurred that the Solicitors' Accounts Rules (SAR) 1935 gave the first statutory recognition of the need for a separate bank account for client money. From this base, the regulatory framework governing the accountability of solicitors has developed until the present position, which requires not only separate bank accounts and accounting records for clients' money but also a review of solicitors' compliance by independent accountants. The SAR, being delegated legislation, have statutory effect. From time to time the SAR are amended by the Society, subject to the approval of the Master of the Rolls. It is vital for solicitors to keep up to date by referring to the Law Society's Gazette and web-site.

THE SOLICITORS' ACCOUNTS RULES

From 1 May 2000, solicitors have had to comply with the SAR 1998, which are contained in Chapter 28 of the eighth edition of the Society's Guide to the Professional Conduct of Solicitors (the Guide). The SAR 1998, which are written in plain English, are a distinct improvement on previous versions of the SAR.

The SAR 1998 purport to integrate the basic rules and general guidance by incorporating the notes into the rules. Rule 2, headed 'Interpretation', states that the SAR are to be interpreted 'in the light of the notes' to the SAR. The passage of time will almost certainly produce legal arguments about the precise wording of the SAR, the relationship of the notes to the rules themselves, and how the phrase 'in the light of' is to be interpreted. There are, in fact, some conflicts between the rules and the notes which we shall look at in due course.

There is also a body of common law in which the courts have interpreted the SAR. The decisions laid down by the courts are binding in accordance with the usual principles of precedent. Solicitors should again keep abreast of new case law, which is often publicised in the Law Society's *Gazette*.

The SAR 1998 are divided into the following parts:

Part A – General

Part B – Client Money, Controlled Trust Money and Operation of a Client Account

Part C – Interest

Part D – Accounting Systems and Records

Part E – Monitoring and Investigation by the Society

Part F – Accountants' Reports

Part G – Commencement

Basic principles

Rule 1 of the SAR 1998 spells out the fundamental principles. Solicitors must:

- Comply with the requirements of Practice Rule 1 regarding integrity, duty to act in the client's best interests and the good repute of themselves and the profession.
- Keep other people's money separate from their own.
- Keep other people's money safe.
- Use a client's or controlled trust money for that client or that trust only.
- Establish and maintain proper systems and controls to ensure compliance with the SAR.
- Keep proper records of clients' and controlled trust money.
- Account for interest on other people's money.
- Co-operate with the Law Society in checking on compliance.
- Deliver the annual accountant's report as required by the SAR.

These principles are indeed welcome, because they assist in the interpretation of the remainder of the SAR and notes. However, there is potential for conflict between the r 1 principles and the other rules and/or notes. For example, a r 1 principle states that solicitors should keep their money separate from other people's money, yet there are exceptions which allow client money to be paid into the office bank account and office money into the client bank account. Another example is the principle that one client's money should not be used for the benefit of another, yet the SAR allow payments out against uncleared cheques, which must involve the (albeit temporary) use of other clients' money. We will draw your attention to such potential problems at relevant points in the text.

We begin with one of the fundamentally important principles – the need to keep other people's money physically separate from a solicitor's money. This raises the question of what is solicitors' money and what is clients' or other people's money? Rule 13 states that money held or received in the course of practice falls into one of three categories:

- client money – money held for a client, and all other money which is not controlled trust money or office money;
- controlled trust money – money held for a controlled trust; or
- office money – money belonging to the solicitor or practice.

The precise definitions of these terms will be explored in more detail later.

A separate bank or building society account

Under r 14(2), the term 'client account' means:

> 'An account of a practice kept at a bank or building society for holding client money and/or controlled trust money.'

Which bank or building society?

The solicitor is free to choose which bank or building society to use for the holding of client money, provided it is:

■ an institution authorised under the Banking Act 1987 (which includes a European authorised institution), the Post Office in the exercise of its powers to provide banking services, or the Bank of England; or

■ recognised as a building society within the meaning of the Building Societies Act 1986 (r 2).

For the sake of convenience, in this book we use the term 'client bank account' to refer to both bank and building society accounts containing client money or controlled trust money.

Under r 14(3), the name (or title) of the client bank account must include:

■ in the case of a sole practitioner, the practitioner's name or the name of the practice;

■ in the case of a partnership, the firm's name;

■ in the case of recognised bodies, the company name or the name of the limited liability partnership (LLP);

■ in the case of in-house solicitors, the principal solicitor or solicitors;

■ in the case of controlled trustees, the name of the firm or the name of the controlled trustees.

In addition, the name or title of the client bank account must include the word 'client' in full, not as an abbreviation (r 14, n (v)). This distinguishes the assets of the clients from those of the solicitor, which may be essential to protect clients' money from the claims of the practice's creditors in the event of the solicitor's death or bankruptcy.

What type of bank account?

Rule 14(4) requires that a client account must be:

■ a bank account at a branch (or a bank's head office) in England and Wales; or

■ a building society deposit (not share) account at a branch (or a society's head office) in England and Wales.

Share accounts are specifically excluded since, although they are operated in precisely the same way as other bank or building society accounts, they are more risky because the account holders are members not depositors, ie they would be the last to be paid out in the event of the winding up of the building society.

For the purposes of the SAR, there are two types of client bank account:

■ A separate designated client bank account, which is a deposit account for a single client's money or a current or deposit account for money held for a single controlled trust which includes in its title a reference to the identity of the client or controlled trust. Note that for some reason it is not allowed to have a designated current account for a single client.

■ A general client bank account, which is any other client bank account. A general client bank account can be seen as a large 'pool' consisting of money belonging to many clients.

An important point is buried in the notes to r 14: client money must be available immediately (unless the client or circumstances clearly indicate otherwise), even if this attracts lower interest rates than could otherwise be obtained. It is hard to say precisely what this means. It may be implied that the funds must be available during normal banking hours. This has several possible, practical implications: for example, is money placed on the overnight money market 'immediately available'? If we were to be pedantic, we could claim that few, if any, bank or building society accounts give complete, unrestricted access to funds on a 24-hour basis. One certain effect of this rule is that those types of bank account which require a period of notice for withdrawals of money (r 14, n (vii)) cannot be used for client money, even though such accounts usually offer higher rates of return.

However, it must be remembered that specific instructions from a client take precedence over the SAR. If solicitors are instructed by their clients to hold client money in a high interest-bearing account requiring 90 days' notice of withdrawal, the instruction must be followed, even though such an account does not meet the definition of a client bank account. The instruction should be given in writing or confirmed in writing by the solicitor to the client (r 16(1)). Solicitors still have to account properly for money held under such instructions.

How many client bank accounts?

A practice may open any number of client bank accounts (r 14, n (iv)). There is no requirement to have a separate bank account for each client. This would be unduly burdensome on even small practices. However, solicitors must open a separate bank account when so instructed by a client and, in addition, we consider that it is sensible, for reasons which will be explained later, for solicitors to open a separate designated account for each controlled trust.

Keeping client money separate is not sufficient to render a complete and fair account to each client. What is also needed is a separate record for each client's matter.

Separate ledger accounts

Rule 32(1) requires solicitors to keep accounting records properly written up to show the solicitor's dealings with client money, controlled trust money and office money relating to a client or controlled trust matter.

Rule 32(2) requires all dealings with client or controlled trust money to be recorded:

■ in a client cash account; and

■ on the client side of a separate client ledger account for each client or controlled trust.

No other entries should be made in these records.

Where separate designated accounts are used:

■ a combined cash account (for general and designated client bank accounts) must be kept to show the total held in separate designated client bank accounts; and

■ a record of the amount held for each client must be made either in a deposit column of a client ledger account or on the client side of a separate client ledger account kept specifically for a separate designated account.

There is an exception (r 32(6)) which allows a solicitor acting for both borrower and lender to put the two clients on one ledger account provided:

■ the funds belonging to each client are clearly identifiable; and

■ the lender is an institution which provides mortgages on standard terms in the normal course of its activities.

Rule 32(4) requires that all office money dealings relating to a client or controlled trust matter must be recorded in an office cash account and on the office side of a client ledger account.

The need to keep separate records of client and controlled trust money and office money means that there will be two ledger accounts for cash (office and client) and similarly two sets of clients' ledger accounts. A set of accounts is known as a 'ledger'. We refer to these two sets of accounts as the 'office ledger' accounts and the 'clients' money ledger' accounts, although other terms may be used in practice. We have chosen the term 'clients' money ledger' to emphasise the fact that only monetary transactions are recorded in this set of accounts.

One method of keeping the records required is to have physically separate ledgers:

OFFICE LEDGER

CLIENT X LEDGER ACCOUNT				
Date	Detail	DR	CR	Balance

CLIENT Y LEDGER ACCOUNT				
Date	Detail	DR	CR	Balance

CASH ACCOUNT				
Date	Detail	DR	CR	Balance

SALARIES ACCOUNT				
Date	Detail	DR	CR	Balance

FEES ACCOUNT				
Date	Detail	DR	CR	Balance

Note

As well as a ledger account for each client and a cash account, there will be ledger accounts for various types of the practice's income, expenditure, assets and liabilities.

CLIENTS' MONEY LEDGER

CLIENT X LEDGER ACCOUNT				
Date	Detail	DR	CR	Balance

CLIENT Y LEDGER ACCOUNT				
Date	Detail	DR	CR	Balance

CASH ACCOUNT				
Date Detail	DR	CR	Balance	

Note

Separate ledger accounts are required for each client and there is a cash account to record the amount in the client bank account(s). There are no other types of account in the clients' money ledger.

In practice, it is more convenient to be able to see at a glance the position of a single client vis-à-vis the office and the client bank account. This is achieved by placing client money columns alongside office columns in the client ledger accounts and by placing client money columns alongside the office cash account. All other ledger accounts are 'office only' accounts. The format for cash and client ledger accounts which we shall adopt is as follows:

CLIENT LEDGER ACCOUNT						
Client:						
Re:						
		Office ledger			*Clients' money ledger*	
Date Detail	DR	CR	Balance	DR	CR	Balance

Note

There is a space for the name of the individual client and also a description of the matter in which the solicitor is acting (as required by the Accounting Guidelines, SAR Appendix 3, para 2.4).

CASH ACCOUNT						
		Office ledger			*Clients' money ledger*	
Date Detail	DR	CR	Balance	DR	CR	Balance

These accounts in a solicitor's practice are operated on the normal double-entry principles already outlined.

In the cash account money from/to a client results in:

> a debit = money IN
>
> a credit = money OUT

Following the double-entry principle, the opposite applies in the client ledger account:

> a debit = money OUT
>
> a credit = money IN

Thus, for receipts of money, the double-entry will be:

> Debit cash account with cash received
>
> Credit the client ledger account of the client from or for whom the money is received

And for payments:

> Credit cash account with payments out
>
> Debit the account of the client for or to whom the payment is made

Receipt of client money

So when a client pays client money to a solicitor, the relevant entries are:

CLIENT LEDGER ACCOUNT						
Client:						
Re:						
		Office ledger			*Clients' money ledger*	
Date	Detail	DR	CR	Balance	DR	CR	Balance
						CLIENT MONEY IN	

Am using ledger A/c or Cash A/c

CASH ACCOUNT						
		Office ledger			*Clients' money ledger*	
Date Detail	DR	CR	Balance	DR	CR	Balance
				CLIENT MONEY IN		

Payment of office money

A solicitor pays money from the firm's own bank account on behalf of a client:

CLIENT LEDGER ACCOUNT						
Client:						
Re:						
		Office ledger			*Clients' money ledger*	
Date Detail	DR	CR	Balance	DR	CR	Balance
	OFFICE MONEY OUT					

CASH ACCOUNT						
		Office ledger			*Clients' money ledger*	
Date Detail	DR	CR	Balance	DR	CR	Balance
		OFFICE MONEY OUT				

The balance on the cash account (clients' money column) is the total amount of money in the client bank account(s) and by virtue of the double-entry principle must always be equal to the total balances on the client ledger accounts (clients' money column). That is, as far as clients' money goes: assets (the money in the bank) = liabilities (to the clients whose money it is). In simple terms, the cash account balance (clients' money column) shows how much the solicitor is holding for clients and the balances on the client ledger accounts (clients' money column) show to whom the money is owed.

Remember that all the accounts for office expenses, income, assets, liabilities and the firm's capital relate to the office alone, ie these accounts have no columns for clients' money.

Key questions

The need to separate, and to keep separate, clients' and solicitors' money raises two key questions whenever a solicitor deals with money (whether by cash, cheque, banker's draft or telegraphic transfer):

1. When money is received, is it office or clients' money?
2. When payments have to be made, should the payment be made from the office or client bank account?

The answers to these questions will determine which bank account is affected and therefore which set of columns (ie office or clients' money) will be used to record the transaction.

Golden rules

If the SAR have been properly followed, the following 'golden rules' will generally apply:

1. The balance in the office column of a client ledger account should never be a credit.
2. The balance in the clients' money column of a client ledger account should never be a debit.

A credit balance in the office column of a client ledger account indicates that client money has been paid into the office bank account, since the credits on that client's ledger account exceed the debits (ie more money has been received for or from that client than has been spent or incurred on that client's behalf).

On the other hand, a debit balance on the clients' money column of a client ledger account is often referred to as an 'overdrawn client account'. This colloquialism has nothing to do with the client bank account per se, but refers to the fact that more money has been paid out of the client bank account for the client than has been received from or for that particular client (ie the debits in the client ledger account, clients' money column, exceed the credits). This is in breach of r 22(5), which aims to prevent the use of one client's money for the benefit of another client.

Our approach in the following chapters mimics that of many computer programs which work on the assumption that a non-zero balance on the client ledger accounts (office column) is a debit balance and a non-zero balance on the clients' money column is a credit. Exceptions to these default settings will be 'flagged' by the computer with the abbreviations DR or CR appearing next to the balance or highlighted in some other way.

EXERCISES

1. You receive a cheque for £100 from a client for whom you have yet to agree a fee or do any work or pay any disbursements. Is this office or client money?

   What are the correct accounting entries in the client ledger account and cash account?

2. You have to make a payment of £250 on behalf of a client for whom you hold no funds. From which bank account must the payment be made, office or client?

   What are the correct accounting entries in the client ledger account and cash account?

3. You receive a cheque for £470 from a client in settlement of a bill of costs previously delivered. Is this office or client money?

   What are the correct accounting entries in the client ledger account and cash account?

4. Explain the main principles behind the SAR.

5. Explain the rationale behind the two 'golden rules'.

Chapter 3

Basic receipts and payments

INTRODUCTION

The key questions introduced in Chapter 2 were aimed at determining into which bank account (office or client) receipts should be deposited and from which bank account payments should be made. This chapter looks at some of the basic issues concerning these questions. The starting point is the different types of money which may be held or received. As mentioned in Chapter 2, all money held or received in the course of practice falls into one of three categories: client money, controlled trust money or office money (for a diagrammatic presentation of the distinctions see the flowchart in Appendix 1).

WHAT IS CLIENT MONEY?

A 'client' is defined as a person for whom the solicitor acts (r 2(2)(e)). Client money therefore includes money held or received:

- as agent, bailee, stakeholder, donee of a power of attorney, liquidator, trustee in bankruptcy or Court of Protection receiver (r 13, n (i)(a));
- for payment of an unpaid professional disbursement (defined in r 2(2)(s) as 'the fees of counsel or other lawyer, or of a professional or other agent or expert instructed by the solicitor'; however, this category is expanded by r 2, n (v) to include fees of interpreters, translators, process servers and estate agents, but not travel agents) (r 13, n (i)(b));
- for payment of stamp duty, Land Registry registration fees, telegraphic transfer fees and court fees (r 13, n (i)(c));
- as a payment on account of costs generally (r 13, n (i)(d));
- as commission paid in respect of a solicitor's client, unless either the client has authorised the solicitor to retain it or the amount is below the £20 de minimis as specified in Practice Rule 10 (r 13, n (i)(e)).

This list is not intended to be exhaustive. There are many types of receipt which are not mentioned but which are obviously client money, for example, a deposit or a mortgage advance for a house purchase. The notes to r 13 seem to be aimed at some of the more tricky kinds of receipt:

■ Money held by solicitors who are trustees of occupational pension schemes will be either client or controlled trust money, depending on the circumstances (r 13, n (iii)).

■ Money held or received in a bank account which is operated jointly with another person outside the practice is client money, though the bank account containing the money is not a client bank account (see the note to r 10) and the record-keeping requirements of the SAR 1998 are limited in application.

■ Money held to the sender's order is client money (r 13, n (v)).

■ A loan or advance to a client which is paid into the client bank account becomes client money (r 13, n (vi)).

■ Trust money is either controlled trust money or client money (r 13, n (vii)).

Accounting for client money

Having determined that a receipt of money is client money, the money needs to be banked promptly. Under r 15, solicitors are obliged to pay client money and controlled trust money into the client bank account *without delay*, a phrase defined in r 2(2)(z) as meaning 'in normal circumstances, either on the day of receipt or on the next working day'.

In addition, the accounting entries need to be made to reflect the receipt of client money. Rule 32, n (i) gives the *strong recommendation* that accounting records are written up at least weekly, even in the smallest practice, and daily in the case of larger firms. This recommendation relates only to those records dealing with clients' matters and would clearly not apply to the office wages or rent account (although for management purposes it may be good practice to draw up the accounts of a practice on a weekly basis).

EXAMPLE

On 5 January 2002, a solicitor receives £100 from Avril on account of costs in relation to the purchase of a flat.

CLIENT LEDGER ACCOUNT						
Client: Avril						
Re: Purchase of flat						
		Office ledger			*Clients' money ledger*	
Date	Detail	DR	CR	Balance	DR	CR	Balance
5.1.02	Cash: on account					100	100

CASH ACCOUNT (extract)						
		Office ledger			Clients' money ledger	
Date	Detail	DR	CR	Balance	DR	CR	Balance
5.1.02	Avril: on account				100		

Note

While the client ledger account shows a balance, no balance appears in the cash account. The reason is that while the client ledger account contains all transactions relating to that client, the cash account in the example shows only the entry which relates to the individual client, Avril. In fact, it is only an extract of the cash account.

It is important to note that if a solicitor wrongly pays Avril's money into the office bank account, the double-entry results in a credit entry (and hence a credit balance) in the client ledger account, office column (the corresponding entry being a debit in the cash account (office column)). A credit balance is obviously a breach not only of the 'golden rule' but also of the SAR, since money paid on account of costs does not belong to the solicitor.

It is clear that the list of categories of client money referred to above is not exhaustive, but perhaps it is unrealistic to expect that such a list could have been devised. This means that more emphasis needs to be placed on common sense and the interpretation of the other two types of money, controlled trust money and office money (see later).

Other payments into the client bank account

The general principle is that only client money or controlled trust money may be paid into a client bank account (r 15(2)). There are, however, exceptions to this principle. Money which is neither client money nor controlled trust money may be deposited into a client bank account if it represents:

1. nominal funds of the solicitor used to open the account (r 15(2)(a)), although this is not usually required in practice as banks will open an account with a nil balance (r 15, n (v));

2. an advance from a solicitor to fund a payment when there are insufficient funds in the client bank account for that client (r 15(2)(b));

3. money paid into the client bank account to replace any sum withdrawn in contravention of r 22 – once paid in, the money becomes client money (r 15(2)(c)); or

4. a sum in lieu of interest which is paid into a client bank account in order to comply with r 24 other than by a payment direct to a client (r 15(2)(d)) – see Chapter 8.

Special cases

Cash and endorsed cheques

Rule 17 identifies categories of client money which need not be paid into the client bank account, including client money received in the form of:

- cash (if it is, without delay, paid in cash in the ordinary course of business to the client or on the client's behalf to a third party); or
- cheques or drafts endorsed over in the ordinary course of business to the client or on the client's behalf to a third party by the solicitor (current banking practice is to issue crossed cheques with 'Account payee' printed between the lines and such crossed cheques cannot be endorsed; however, there may be some banks which still provide customers with cheques which are not crossed).

These exceptions relate only to the physical act of depositing the cash or cheque into the client bank account. Even though the money itself is never actually paid into the client bank account, the solicitor has *handled* client money and must make appropriate accounting entries in the client ledger account and client cash account to record both the receipt and the paying over of the money (r 17, n (ii)).

EXAMPLE

A firm acts for a client, Claire, in a sale and purchase of properties. On 20 March 2002 the buyer's solicitor sends the firm a cheque for £10,000 with Claire's instruction that it is to be endorsed over to the seller's solicitor. The cash and client ledger accounts reflect the above as follows. First the receipt of the cheque is recorded:

CLIENT LEDGER ACCOUNT							
Client: Claire							
Re: Sale & purchase							
		Office ledger			*Clients' money ledger*		
Date	Detail	DR	CR	Balance	DR	CR	Balance
20.3.02	Cash: cheque received					10,000	10,000

CASH ACCOUNT (extract)							
		Office ledger			*Clients' money ledger*		
Date	Detail	DR	CR	Balance	DR	CR	Balance
20.3.02	Cash: cheque received				10,000		

Then the fact that the cheque is endorsed and handed over to the seller's solicitors is recorded:

CLIENT LEDGER ACCOUNT							
Client: Claire							
Re: Sale & purchase							
		Office ledger			Clients' money ledger		
Date	Detail	DR	CR	Balance	DR	CR	Balance
20.3.02	Cash: cheque received					10,000	10,000
	Cash: cheque endorsed				10,000		0

CASH ACCOUNT (extract)							
		Office ledger			Clients' money ledger		
Date	Detail	DR	CR	Balance	DR	CR	Balance
20.3.02	Claire: cheque received				10,000		
	Claire: cheque endorsed					10,000	

It may be useful to indicate to anyone checking the cash records (eg those required to perform the monthly comparisons of the cash book/account with the bank statements: see Chapter 9) that the two entries in the cash account will not appear on the bank statement. An example of the sort of indication which might be used is given below:

CASH ACCOUNT (extract)							
		Office ledger			Clients' money ledger		
Date	Detail	DR	CR	Balance	DR	CR	Balance
20.3.02	Claire: cheque received				10,000¢		
	Claire: cheque endorsed					10,000¢	

Money withheld on client's instruction

A solicitor need not pay into the client bank account client money which the client instructs is to be paid into the client's own personal bank account or a bank account of another designated by the client in writing or acknowledged by the solicitor in writing (r 17 (c)).

WHAT IS CONTROLLED TRUST MONEY?

Controlled trust money is money held or received for a controlled trust defined in r 2(h) as arising when:

- A solicitor is a sole trustee or trustee only with one or more of his or her partners or employees.

- A solicitor who is a director or partner of a recognised body is the sole trustee or co-trustee only with one or more of the recognised body's other officers or employees or with the recognised body itself. (A recognised body refers to an incorporated firm or LLP. Before commencing practice, every incorporated firm must obtain the recognition of the Council of the Law Society as being a suitable body to undertake the provision of legal services (see r 2(1) of the Solicitors' Incorporated Practice Rules 1988).)

- A registered foreign lawyer who is a partner in a multinational partnership is the sole trustee or co-trustee only with one or more of the partnership's partners or employees.

- A registered foreign lawyer who is the director of a recognised body is, by virtue of practising as a director of the recognised body, the sole trustee or co-trustee only with one or more of the recognised body's other officers or employees or with the recognised body itself.

- A recognised body is the sole trustee of a trust, or co-trustee only with one or more of the recognised body's officers, employees or partners.

A controlled trustee is a trustee of a controlled trust.

Rule 13, n (iv) highlights the fact that the definition of a controlled trust derives from statute but can give rise to anomalies, for example, when a partner or assistant solicitor or a consultant acts as sole trustee, he or she will be a controlled trustee, whereas two or more assistant solicitors or consultants acting as trustees are not controlled trustees.

WHAT IS OFFICE MONEY?

Office money is money which belongs to the solicitor or to the practice (r 13 (c)). Office money includes:

- money held or received in connection with the running of the practice (r 3, n (xi)(a)), for example, PAYE and VAT on the firm's fees; other examples include partners' capital contributions and receipts from sales of assets;

- interest on general client account (r 13, n (xi) (b));

- amounts received:

  - to pay the firm's fees, a bill having been delivered (r 13, n (xi)(c)(A));

  - to reimburse the firm for disbursements paid from the office bank account (r 13, n (xi)(c)(B));

- to put the firm in funds to pay a disbursement for which a liability has been incurred but not yet paid, excluding unpaid professional disbursements (r 13, n (xi)(c)(C) but see one option under r 19); and

- money paid for or towards an agreed fee (r 13, n (xi)(c)(D), an agreed fee is defined in r 19(5)).

EXAMPLE

Money received in respect of disbursements already paid out of the office bank account must be paid into the office bank account.

On 8 January 2002, a solicitor received £100 from Brian in respect of a doctor's fee already paid out from the office bank account on 6 January 2002. The payment of the doctor's fee would be recorded thus:

CLIENT LEDGER ACCOUNT							
Client: Brian							
Re: Personal injury							
		Office ledger			Clients' money ledger		
Date	Detail	DR	CR	Balance	DR	CR	Balance
6.1.02	Cash: doctor's fee	100		100			

CASH ACCOUNT (extract)							
		Office ledger			Clients' money ledger		
Date	Detail	DR	CR	Balance	DR	CR	Balance
6.1.02	Brian: doctor's fee		100				

The receipt of the reimbursement by Brian would be recorded as:

CLIENT LEDGER ACCOUNT							
Client: Brian							
Re: Personal injury							
		Office ledger			Clients' money ledger		
Date	Detail	DR	CR	Balance	DR	CR	Balance
6.1.02	Cash: doctor's fee	100		100			
8.1.02	Cash: disbursement: from you		100	0			

CASH ACCOUNT (extract)							
		Office ledger			*Clients' money ledger*		
Date	Detail	DR	CR	Balance	DR	CR	Balance
6.1.02	Brian: doctor's fee		100				
8.1.02	Brian: disbursement	100					

Money held in a client bank account after the solicitor has completed the work and a bill has been delivered becomes office money and, under (r 19(3)), must be transferred from the client bank account to the office bank account within 14 days.

Money received for or on behalf of a principal for whom the firm is acting

A solicitor cannot be his or her own client. However, such money may be client money if the firm also acts for the lender or if the firm is acting jointly for the principal's spouse (who is not otherwise connected to the firm) in connection with a matter or if the firm acts for an assistant solicitor, consultant or non-solicitor employee or a director of a company or member of an LLP in the case of a recognised body (r 13, n (xii)(c)).

Payments to legal aid practitioners

Payments from the Legal Services Commission may be paid into an office bank account following an instruction from the Commission (r 21(1)(a)).

A receipt of money for costs or a mixed receipt (comprising both office and client money) may be paid into an office bank account, even though part of it is an advance payment of fees or disbursements or relates to unpaid professional disbursements, provided that all money for unpaid disbursements is transferred from the office bank account to the client bank account (or the disbursement is paid) within 14 days of receipt (r 21(1)). The initial receipt of the money is recorded in the office column of the client ledger account for the client whose matter is being funded or the account of the Legal Services Commission (r 32, n (v)).

The Commission requires solicitors to report recovery of costs previously paid by the Commission (r 21, n (iv)). Rule 21(2) requires solicitors who have been reimbursed by the Commission and who subsequently recover their costs or professional disbursements from a third party, to:

■ pay the entire sum into a client bank account;

■ retain in a client bank account a sum equivalent to the Commission's payments;

■ transfer to an office bank account the amount belonging to the solicitor within 14 days of sending a report containing details of the third party payment to the Commission.

■ The sum retained in the client bank account must be either recorded in the individual client's ledger account but identified as belonging to the Commission or recorded in a ledger account in the name of the Commission with a reference to the individual client and kept in the client bank account until notification from the Commission that it has recouped the relevant sum by deduction from a subsequent legal aid payment, after which the sum may be transferred to the office bank account within 14 days of such notification.

Unpaid professional disbursements

Money received by the solicitor for an unpaid professional disbursement may be paid into the office account (r 17(d) and (e)). Rule 19(1)(b) provides that, by the end of the second working day following receipt, either the disbursement is paid or the money is transferred from the office bank account to the client bank account. Similarly, a receipt of money from the Legal Services Commission to pay a solicitor's costs may be deposited in the office bank account provided any amounts in relation to unpaid disbursements are transferred into the client bank account or the disbursement is paid within 14 days of receipt (r 21(1)(b)).

Council authority

Money may be withheld from a client bank account on the written authorisation of the Council of the Law Society (r 17(f)).

Money 'held to order'

A cheque or draft sent to a solicitor on terms that it is 'to be held to the sender's order' should not be paid into the client bank account until the sender's consent has been given (r 13, n (v)(b)). In contrast, a telegraphic transfer on similar terms *must* be entered in the client money columns of the cash account and the client ledger account, since the money itself has been paid *directly* into the bank account.

A joint bank account

The SAR 1998 have a limited application to money held or received by solicitors jointly with the client, or with another solicitors' practice or with another third party (r 10(1)). A joint bank account is not a client bank account but the money in the joint bank account is client money (r 10).

Client's own bank account

When a solicitor operates a client's own bank account (for example, under a power of attorney) the money in this account is *not* client money (r 13, n (ix)). However, solicitors in this position are subject to a limited application of the SAR 1998 relating to record-keeping and monitoring by reporting accountants.

Third-party cheques

A third-party cheque received by the solicitor and forwarded to the client is not client money (because the money is never under the solicitor's control) and so entries should not appear in the DR or CR columns of the ledger accounts (r 32, n (iii)). However, a memorandum entry may be made in the details column of the client ledger account indicating that the cheque has been received and handed over; alternatively, a note on the file may be the only record.

EXAMPLE

On 22 March 2002, a firm acting in a debt collection case for ABC & Co receives a cheque for £200 made payable to ABC & Co from one of their debtors, Late Pay Ltd. The cheque is forwarded to ABC & Co.

CLIENT LEDGER ACCOUNT							
Client: ABC & Co							
Re: Debt collection							
		Office ledger			*Clients' money ledger*		
Date	Detail	DR	CR	Balance	DR	CR	Balance
22.3.02	£200 cheque received from Late Pay Ltd payable & forwarded to ABC						

CASH ACCOUNT (extract)							
		Office ledger			*Clients' money ledger*		
Date	Detail	DR	CR	Balance	DR	CR	Balance

PAYMENTS OUT OF THE CLIENT BANK ACCOUNT

Rule 22 lays down the conditions which must be met before any client money and controlled trust money may be withdrawn from a client bank account. The payment must be:

- properly required for a payment to or on behalf of the client;
- properly required for payment of a disbursement on behalf of a client;
- properly required in full or partial reimbursement of money spent by the solicitor on behalf of the client;
- transferred to another client bank account;
- withdrawn on the client's instructions (in writing or confirmed in writing by the solicitor);
- to refund the solicitor for an advance no longer required;
- which has wrongly been paid into the client bank account; or
- withdrawn on the written authorisation of the Society.

Paying a disbursement for a client

EXAMPLE

On 1 February 2002, a solicitor pays £100 on behalf of Ernest, from whom he has already received, on 5 January 2002, £100 in advance.

The payment in advance will be recorded as:

CLIENT LEDGER ACCOUNT							
Client: Ernest							
Re: Litigation							
		Office ledger			Clients' money ledger		
Date	Detail	DR	CR	Balance	DR	CR	Balance
5.1.02	Cash: on account					100	100

CASH ACCOUNT (extract)							
		Office ledger			Clients' money ledger		
Date	Detail	DR	CR	Balance	DR	CR	Balance
5.1.02	Ernest: on account				100		

Now the entries for recording the payment of the disbursement from the client bank account are:

CLIENT LEDGER ACCOUNT							
Client: Ernest							
Re: Litigation							
		Office ledger			Clients' money ledger		
Date	Detail	DR	CR	Balance	DR	CR	Balance
5.1.02	Cash: on account					100	100
1.2.02	Cash: disbursement				100		0

CASH ACCOUNT (extract)						
		Office ledger			*Clients' money ledger*	
Date	Detail	DR	CR	Balance	DR	CR	Balance
5.1.02	Ernest: on account				100		
1.2.02	Ernest: disbursement					100	

Withdrawing office money from client bank account

The Society has long been concerned that some solicitors have been tardy in withdrawing their fees from the client bank account. There are a number of possible reasons for this reluctance to take money to which solicitors are entitled: some may have considered that they were being prudent or cautious in leaving undrawn fees in the client bank account as a cushion against future shortfalls on the account of that client or to cover other unexpected deficiencies or contingencies; others may have been able to obtain a higher rate of interest on their client bank account than their *in credit* office bank account and so were better off the longer they left their own money in the general client bank account. Whatever the reason, this practice is now expressly prohibited by r 19(3), which states that once a solicitor has sent a bill or other written notification of costs, the money in the client bank account becomes office money and must be transferred into the office bank account within 14 days (see also r 19, n (xii)). Of course, it is in the commercial interests of solicitors to withdraw their costs as soon as possible, provided that they are legally entitled to do so. The transfer from client to office account should be for the precise amount of the bill and should not exceed the amount held for that particular client; round-sum transfers are not permitted (r 19, n (x)).

Rule 23(3) lays down that withdrawal of money from the client bank account in favour of the solicitor should only be by either:

■ a cheque to the solicitor or practice, or

■ a bank transfer to an office bank account or to the solicitor's personal bank account.

The withdrawal must not be made in cash.

For the accounting entries to record transfers of money between office and client bank accounts, see Chapter 5.

Writing off small balances

Small balances held for clients whose address is no longer known may not be 'written off' (ie transferred from client to office bank account) without the Law Society Council's permission (r 22(1)(h)).

Payments from petty cash

Petty cash refers to notes and coins kept in the office. Petty cash is office money, since all client cash should have been banked without delay. The petty cash ledger account therefore has no columns for client money.

EXAMPLE

On 1 March 2002, a solicitor pays swearing fees of £10 on behalf of a client, Gregory, out of the petty cash box into which £100 was deposited on 31 January.

First record the £100 float being paid into the petty cash box from the main bank account:

PETTY CASH ACCOUNT (extract)				
			Office ledger	
Date	Detail	DR	CR	Balance
31.1.02	Cash: deposit from main account	100		100

CASH ACCOUNT (extract)							
		Office ledger			*Clients' money ledger*		
Date	Detail	DR	CR	Balance	DR	CR	Balance
31.1.02	Petty cash: deposit into petty cash		100				

Then record the payment from the petty cash box of the swearing fee on behalf of Gregory:

CLIENT LEDGER ACCOUNT							
Client: Gregory							
Re: Probate							
		Office ledger			*Clients' money ledger*		
Date	Detail	DR	CR	Balance	DR	CR	Balance
1.3.02	Petty cash: swearing fee	10		10			

PETTY CASH ACCOUNT (extract)				
			Office ledger	
Date	Detail	DR	CR	Balance
31.1.02	Cash: deposit from main account	100		100
1.3.02	Gregory: swearing fee		10	90

CASH ACCOUNT (extract)						
		Office ledger			Clients' money ledger		
Date	Detail	DR	CR	Balance	DR	CR	Balance
31.1.02	Petty cash: deposit into petty cash		100				

Who may authorise the withdrawal of money?

Rule 23(1) states that withdrawals from the client bank account may be made only where a specific authority has been signed by at least one of the following:

- a solicitor who holds a current practising certificate;
- a Fellow of the Institute of Legal Executives of at least three years standing employed by such a solicitor;
- in the case of an office dealing solely with conveyancing, a licensed conveyancer who is employed by such a solicitor; or
- a registered foreign lawyer who is a partner or director or member of the practice.

Other employees of the practice may authorise withdrawals if money is simply being moved between general client bank accounts at the same bank or building society.

EXERCISES

1. Give five examples of receipts of client money.
2. When may a solicitor not be obliged to pay client money into the client bank account?
3. When is a solicitor not obliged to record receipts of client money in a client ledger account and cash book (or similar records)?
4. When may money be withdrawn from the client bank account?
5. Who may authorise withdrawal of client money?
6. By what means may a solicitor withdraw client money in settlement of a bill delivered to a client?

Chapter 4

Fees, VAT, abatements and bad debts

INTRODUCTION

Accounting for solicitors' fees often causes some difficulty at first, not least because of the terminology used. Historically, solicitors have been reluctant to give the impression that they were in practice in order to make money. The use of the term 'costs' is now widespread, but it is very misleading to a lay person. In everyday parlance, 'cost' denotes some form of expense incurred. Referring to solicitors' costs, therefore, gives the misleading impression that solicitors simply recover the expenses incurred and are not charging fees to make a profit. The term 'profit costs' is perhaps an improvement but may also cause confusion as a result of the juxtaposition of two contradictory terms. We feel that the most appropriate term is 'fees'. However, students should note the particular meanings attached to the terms 'costs' and 'fees' under the SAR 1998:

■ 'costs' means a solicitor's fees *and* disbursements; and

■ 'fees' means the solicitor's own charges or profit costs (including any VAT element).

A second problem for students to overcome is the notion that accounting entries have to be made to record the delivery of a bill even though there is no movement of money. The entries are required to recognise the debts due to solicitors from their clients.

EXAMPLE

On 19 April 2002, a solicitor delivers a bill of £100 for work in drawing up a will on behalf of a client, Colin:

CLIENT LEDGER ACCOUNT						
Client: Colin						
Re: Will						
		Office ledger			Clients' money ledger	
Date	Detail	DR	CR	Balance	DR	CR	Balance
19.4.02	Fees	100		100			

FEES ACCOUNT (extract)				
			Office ledger	
Date	Detail	DR	CR	Balance
19.4.02	Colin		100	

Note

An accounting entry is made to record the establishment of the debt by the client to the solicitor even though no money has been received.

Then on 19 May 2002, Colin pays £100:

CLIENT LEDGER ACCOUNT							
Client: Colin							
Re: Will							
		Office ledger			*Clients' money ledger*		
Date	Detail	DR	CR	Balance	DR	CR	Balance
19.4.02	Fees	100		100			
19.5.02	Cash: fees		100	0			

CASH ACCOUNT (extract)							
		Office ledger			*Clients' money ledger*		
Date	Detail	DR	CR	Balance	DR	CR	Balance
19.5.02	Colin: fees	100					

FEES ACCOUNT (extract)				
			Office ledger	
Date	Detail	DR	CR	Balance
19.4.02	Colin		100	

Note

■ the double-entry to record the receipt of the fee is to debit the office cash account and credit the relevant client ledger account;
■ no entry is made in the fees account on receipt of the money;

- as the accounting period progresses, the balance on the fees account continues to grow as more bills are delivered;
- at the end of the year, the balance on the fees account is taken to the profit and loss account and represents the total value of all bills delivered (see Chapter 11).

Agreed fees

An 'agreed fee' is a fee that is fixed; it is not a fee that can be varied upwards, nor one that is dependent on the completion of a transaction (r 19(5)). Money for or towards an agreed fee is office money and must be paid into the office bank account, (r 19(5)). The agreement by the client to pay a fixed fee establishes the client's debt to the solicitor and accounting entries need to be made at the date of the agreement even though no bill has been delivered. Although an agreed fee must be evidenced in writing (r 19(5)), unlike other fees, the solicitor is not required to deliver a bill, although the written evidence of the agreement should be kept as a written notification of costs (r 19, n (xiii)).

EXAMPLE

On 2 April 2002, a solicitor agrees to provide Dawn with advice in a matrimonial matter for an agreed fee of £200. Dawn pays the solicitor £200 on 12 April 2002, although she has yet to receive a bill.

First we need to record the agreement of the fee. This will produce a debit in the client ledger account (office column) and a credit in the fees account. These entries are necessary to prevent a credit balance occurring on the client ledger balance (office column) when the client pays. Furthermore, the entries are needed for VAT purposes, since the VAT point for agreed fees is the date of the agreement (see later for accounting entries for VAT).

CLIENT LEDGER ACCOUNT							
Client: Dawn							
Re: Matrimonial							
		Office ledger			*Clients' money ledger*		
Date	Detail	DR	CR	Balance	DR	CR	Balance
2.4.02	Fees: agreed fee	100		100			

FEES ACCOUNT (extract)				
		Office ledger		
Date	Detail	DR	CR	Balance
2.4.02	Dawn: agreed fee		100	

Then the receipt of the money needs to be recorded: debit the cash account (office column), credit the client ledger account (office column):

CLIENT LEDGER ACCOUNT							
Client: Dawn							
Re: Matrimonial							
		Office ledger			Clients' money ledger		
Date	Detail	DR	CR	Balance	DR	CR	Balance
2.4.02	Fees: agreed fee	100		100			
12.4.02	Cash: fees		100	0			

CASH ACCOUNT (extract)							
		Office ledger			Clients' money ledger		
Date	Detail	DR	CR	Balance	DR	CR	Balance
12.4.02	Dawn: fees	100					

FEES ACCOUNT (extract)				
		Office ledger		
Date	Detail	DR	CR	Balance
2.4.02	Dawn: agreed fee		100	

VAT

Businesses with an annual turnover in excess of a threshold specified by statute are obliged to register with Customs and Excise. The turnover threshold has tended to change with each new Budget, but is strictly applied. In *Ayr Solicitors Property Centre* [1986] 2 BVC 208, 112, solicitors unsuccessfully argued that they should incur no penalty for failing to notify their liability to register for VAT since they were only £102 over the VAT threshold. The tribunal decided this was irrelevant; however, the penalty can now be mitigated (VAT Act 1994, s 67(8)).

A VAT-registered business is referred to as a 'registered trader'. Each registered trader must (subject to certain exceptions) add VAT (generally $17\frac{1}{2}\%$ at present) to the value of every supply of goods or services made for a consideration. The VAT added to the value of the supply is known as the 'output tax'. Registered traders are entitled to deduct from their total output tax the VAT incurred for goods and services which they have bought in, their 'input tax'. Every quarter (or, by election, every month), the registered trader has to submit a VAT return, along with a payment to the Customs and Excise of the net balance (ie output VAT less input VAT).

For example, a registered trader buys in goods/services for a total of £100 on which VAT of £17.50 has been charged, then sells the goods or delivers a service for £400 plus

VAT of £70. This trader has added £300 of value to the original goods/services. Since the principle of VAT is that the tax is charged on the added value, the trader's liability to the Customs and Excise is £52.50 (being $17\frac{1}{2}\%$ of the £300 value added or shown by the VAT return: £70 output tax less £17.50 input tax).

EXAMPLE

If we introduce VAT to the example of Colin above:

CLIENT LEDGER ACCOUNT

Client: Colin

Re: Will

		Office ledger			Clients' money ledger		
Date	Detail	DR	CR	Balance	DR	CR	Balance
19.4.02	Fees	100.00		100.00			
	VAT	17.50		117.50			

FEES ACCOUNT (extract)

		Office ledger		
Date	Detail	DR	CR	Balance
19.4.02	Colin		100	

VAT ACCOUNT (extract)

		Office ledger		
Date	Detail	DR	CR	Balance
19.4.02	Colin		17.50	

Note

- VAT appears as a separate line item in the client ledger account since the credit entry for the £17.50 is in the ledger account for VAT not the ledger account for fees.
- Generally the balance on the VAT account will be a credit, representing the solicitor's liability to the Customs and Excise which should be discharged when the solicitor makes the VAT return at the end of the quarter.
- With the addition of VAT, the debt due to the solicitor is increased. The client is expected to pay the full amount, namely, £117.50.

On receipt of this amount the entries will be:

CLIENT LEDGER ACCOUNT							
Client: Colin							
Re: Will							
		Office ledger			*Clients' money ledger*		
Date	Detail	DR	CR	Balance	DR	CR	Balance
19.4.02	Fees	100.00		100.00			
	VAT	17.50		117.50			
19.5.02	Cash: fees		117.50	0			

CASH ACCOUNT (extract)							
		Office ledger			*Clients' money ledger*		
Date	Detail	DR	CR	Balance	DR	CR	Balance
19.4.02	Colin: fees	117.50					

FEES ACCOUNT (extract)				
			Office ledger	
Date	Detail	DR	CR	Balance
19.4.02	Colin		100	

VAT ACCOUNT (extract)				
			Office ledger	
Date	Detail	DR	CR	Balance
19.4.02	Colin		17.50	

Note

In general, on receipt of the debt from the client, there is no entry in the fees account or the VAT account. An exception to this rule occurs when solicitors elect to account for VAT on the cash basis (ie they are only liable to pay Customs and Excise VAT on services for which they have actually received payment). If the solicitor acting in the above case for Colin were on the cash basis for VAT purposes, the VAT entries would be made, not on 19 April (the date of the bill), but on the date of receipt of Colin's remittance (see below). The cash basis requires separate columns in the records of cash payments and receipts (or some other similar means of analysis) in order to identify the VAT element from which the client and fees account are posted.

Zero-rated and exempt services

Exports are zero-rated. Services to overseas clients are treated as exports of goods, so solicitors charge their foreign clients VAT at 0%. If all of a solicitor's services were zero-rated, the solicitor would be liable to pay no VAT but would be able to claim a deduction for input VAT on goods and services received. The solicitor in this position will therefore expect to receive repayments of VAT.

In contrast, certain services are exempt from VAT (eg those of a doctor). An exempt trader can neither charge output VAT nor reclaim any input VAT.

The VAT point

The VAT point for most transactions is the date on the invoice, although for agreed fees it is the date of the agreement. Traders have to account for VAT charged on all transactions made within the VAT accounting period, usually a quarter, less any input tax incurred in that period. Payment has to be made to Customs and Excise within one month of the end of the quarter. Delays in mailing the return may incur penalties. In *Jones* [1991] BVC 1, 337, the solicitor mailed the VAT return on the last day possible. The solicitor unsuccessfully argued that putting the return in the mail within the time limits was sufficient.

VAT returns should be submitted on time even if this means estimating certain amounts. In *Messrs Oldens* [1989] 4 BVC 1,447, Customs and Excise successfully penalised solicitors for late filing (their return was one day late) after their computer system malfunctioned. The tribunal decided that they should have done something other than simply delay the filing; for example, they could have estimated the amount owed.

Having to account for the VAT as at the date of the bill may cause severe cash flow problems when clients fail to pay on time or fail to pay at all. Any registered trader offering a continuing service can elect to substitute a different date from the date on the invoice – the alternative is normally the date the invoice is paid, ie it is a cash-based system. Solicitors can benefit considerably from being able to account to Customs and Excise for the output tax on fees when the fees are paid. However, Customs and Excise may withdraw authorisation for the cash accounting scheme for repeated delays in filing returns (*Trischler* [1991] BVC 1, 309).

COMMISSIONS

Solicitors who, with the client's agreement under Practice Rule 10, receive commissions in respect of clients' affairs (eg life assurance commissions) can adopt the policy of netting this commission off against the fee charged. VAT is then calculated on the net, ie lower, sum, with obvious benefit to the client.

ABATEMENTS

The term 'abatement' is used to describe an agreed reduction in fees after an initial bill of fees has been sent to a client.

Accounting for abatements involves partial reversal of the original entries (including VAT charged). Since it is useful for management purposes to identify how much has been allowed for abatements, it is usually appropriate to open a separate abatements account (which will be treated as an expense account in the profit and loss account) rather than simply to debit the fees account.

EXAMPLE

On 1 May 2002, Boverton & Co send a bill for £1,000 to their client, Alma, for employment advice. Alma objects to the amount of the bill, and after prolonged discussion, on 3 September 2002, Boverton & Co eventually agree to a 20% reduction in the fee and send Alma the necessary credit note. The accounting entries would be:

CLIENT LEDGER ACCOUNT

Client: Alma

Re: Employment advice

		Office ledger			Clients' money ledger		
Date	Detail	DR	CR	Balance	DR	CR	Balance
1.5.02	Fees	1,000		1,000			
	VAT	175		1,175			
3.9.02	Abatement: of fees		200				
	VAT		35	940			

FEES ACCOUNT (extract)

Date	Detail	DR	CR	Balance
1.5.02	Alma		1,000	

ABATEMENT ACCOUNT (extract)

Date	Detail	DR	CR	Balance
3.9.02	Alma	200		

VAT ACCOUNT (extract)

Date	Detail	DR	CR	Balance
1.5.02	Alma: fees		175	
3.9.02	Alma: abatement	35		

Note

The reduction in the fee is credited to Alma's account and debited not to the fees account but to a separate abatements account. This is so that, at the end of the year, when the firm's financial statements are drawn up there will be a separate record of the total fees billed (the final balance on the fees account) and the total of the credit notes sent out. This provides more useful information than if only a net figure (fees less abatements) is available.

BAD DEBTS

One of the risks of doing business on credit is that clients, having received the solicitor's services, may be unable to pay their debts. To reflect the commercial reality of this situation debts which cannot be, or are unlikely to be, recovered should not continue to be shown as an asset but instead should be written off.

EXAMPLE

A solicitor acts for a client, Worthless Ltd, and on 2 April 2002 renders a bill of £3,000 + VAT for advice on a company matter. On 4 July 2002, it is discovered that the company has been put into liquidation and that there is no prospect of the unsecured creditors receiving any payment.

CLIENT LEDGER ACCOUNT

Client: Worthless Ltd

Re: Company advice

		Office ledger			Clients' money ledger		
Date	Detail	DR	CR	Balance	DR	CR	Balance
2.4.02	Fees	3,000		3,000			
	VAT	525		3,525			
4.7.02	Bad debts		3,000				
	VAT suspense		525	0			

FEES ACCOUNT (extract)

Date	Detail	DR	CR	Balance
2.4.02	Worthless		3,000	

BAD DEBTS ACCOUNT (extract)

Date	Detail	DR	CR	Balance
4.7.02	Worthless	3,000		

VAT ACCOUNT (extract)				
Date	Detail	DR	CR	Balance
2.4.02	Worthless fees		525	

VAT SUSPENSE ACCOUNT (extract)				
			Office ledger	
Date	Detail	DR	CR	Balance
4.7.02	Worthless: bad debt	525		

The VAT on a bad debt can only be reclaimed after six months have elapsed from the date of the invoice, provided the debt has been written off for accounting purposes and the VAT on the original invoice has been remitted to Customs. Contrast this with the treatment where a debt is provided for rather than written off (see Chapter 12) – the effects on the profit and loss account and balance sheet are the same but the VAT implications are different.

EXERCISES

1. What is the double-entry for recording the delivery to a client of a bill of £400 assuming that: (a) no VAT is chargeable; and (b) VAT is to be added?

2. What does the balance on the fees account represent?

3. What is the usual accounting period for VAT purposes?

4. A client ledger account shows a debit balance of £235 in relation to a bill and VAT. The debtor has now been declared bankrupt and the debt must be written off. What is the double-entry to record the writing off of the debt, including VAT?

5. A solicitor bills a client for £4,700 inclusive of VAT. The client complains about the amount of the bill and the solicitor agrees to reduce the fee by £1,000 plus VAT. What are the accounting entries to record the abatement?

6. What is the relevance of the VAT point of any transaction?

ADDITIONAL READING

■ Phelps, J and Gizzi, J *VAT for Solicitors* (London: Butterworths, 2nd edn, 1993).

Chapter 5

Transfers and split money

INTRODUCTION

Accounting for transfers of money between client and office bank accounts often causes difficulties simply because there are two sets of double entries: one set in the clients' money ledger columns and one set in the office columns.

TRANSFERS BETWEEN CLIENT AND OFFICE BANK ACCOUNTS

Client money may be transferred from the client bank account to the office bank account in order to reimburse the solicitor for disbursements paid out for the client from the office bank account (r 22(1)).

EXAMPLE

On 1 June 2002, Xavier deposits £1,000 with a firm on account of costs in bringing an action for alleged fraud. On 18 June 2002, the firm pays £800 in disbursements for expert witness evidence from the office bank account. On 30 June 2002, the firm transfers the balance on the client bank account to the office bank account.

CLIENT LEDGER ACCOUNT							
Client: Xavier							
Re: Fraud allegation							
			Office ledger			Clients' money ledger	
Date	Detail	DR	CR	Balance	DR	CR	Balance
1.6.02	Cash: on account					1,000	1,000

CASH ACCOUNT (extract)							
		Office ledger			*Clients' money ledger*		
Date	Detail	DR	CR	Balance	DR	CR	Balance
1.6.02	Xavier: on account				1,000		

Then the payment of the fees of the expert witness from the office bank account needs to be recorded:

CLIENT LEDGER ACCOUNT							
Client: Xavier							
Re: Fraud allegation							
		Office ledger			*Clients' money ledger*		
Date	Detail	DR	CR	Balance	DR	CR	Balance
1.6.02	Cash: on account					1,000	1,000
18.6.02	Cash: expert witness	800		800			1,000

CASH ACCOUNT (extract)							
		Office ledger			*Clients' money ledger*		
Date	Detail	DR	CR	Balance	DR	CR	Balance
1.6.02	Xavier: on account				1,000		
18.6.02	Xavier: expert witness		800				

Finally, the transfer of funds from client to office bank account is recorded. Because this often causes so much confusion, let us take the transfer in two stages. First, the money, £800, is taken out of the client bank account:

CLIENT LEDGER ACCOUNT							
Client: Xavier							
Re: Fraud allegation							
		Office ledger			*Clients' money ledger*		
Date	Detail	DR	CR	Balance	DR	CR	Balance
1.6.02	Cash: on account					1,000	1,000
18.6.02	Cash: expert witness	800		800			1,000
30.6.02	Cash: TFR: disbursements (OUT of client bank account)				800		200

CASH ACCOUNT (extract)							
		Office ledger			Clients' money ledger		
Date	Detail	DR	CR	Balance	DR	CR	Balance
1.6.02	Xavier: on account				1,000		
18.6.02	Xavier: expert witness		800				
30.6.02	Xavier: TFR: disbursements (OUT of client bank account)					800	

For the moment, £800 is suspended in mid-air: it has come out of the client bank account but has yet to descend into the office bank account. To record the receipt of the money into the office bank account, the following entries are required:

CLIENT LEDGER ACCOUNT							
Client: Xavier							
Re: Fraud allegation							
		Office ledger			Clients' money ledger		
Date	Detail	DR	CR	Balance	DR	CR	Balance
1.6.02	Cash: on account					1,000	1,000
18.6.02	Cash: expert witness	800		800			1,000
30.6.02	Cash: TFR: disbursements (OUT of client bank account and IN to office bank account)		800	0	800		200

CASH ACCOUNT (extract)							
		Office ledger			Clients' money ledger		
Date	Detail	DR	CR	Balance	DR	CR	Balance
1.6.02	Xavier: on account				1,000		
18.6.02	Xavier: expert witness		800				
30.6.02	Xavier: TFR: disbursements (OUT of client bank account and IN to office bank account)	800				800	

In practice, transfers may appear on the same line of the ledger account, namely:

CLIENT LEDGER ACCOUNT							
Client: Xavier							
Re: Fraud allegation							
		Office ledger			*Clients' money ledger*		
Date	Detail	DR	CR	Balance	DR	CR	Balance
1.6.02	Cash: on account					1,000	1,000
18.6.02	Cash: expert witness		800				
30.6.02	Xavier: TFR: disbursements	800				800	

CASH ACCOUNT (extract)							
		Office ledger			*Clients' money ledger*		
Date	Detail	DR	CR	Balance	DR	CR	Balance
1.6.02	Xavier: on account				1,000		
18.6.02	Xavier: expert witness		800				
30.6.02	Xavier: TFR: disbursements	800				800	

The above style of presentation is the one which we prefer and which we use in later examples.

Similar client-to-office transfers would be required to take office money out of the client bank account in order to comply with r 22 (3) in respect of:

- the solicitor's money used to open or maintain the account (under r 15(2)(a));
- money properly required to pay the solicitor's costs (under r 19(2) and (3));
- the removal of office money paid into the client bank account (under r 19(1)(c));
- the removal of the non-client balance of mixed receipts paid into the client bank account (under r 20(2)(b)); or
- the correction of an error involving the payment into the client bank account of non-client money, for example, interest on the general client bank account (as required by r 22(4)).

Excess withdrawals

Rule 22(5) authorises the withdrawal of money from a general client bank account only to the extent that money is held for a particular client or controlled trust. To effect a withdrawal in excess of money held for an individual client would entail using other clients' money and is a serious breach of the SAR. In reality, complexities arise because of the time it takes for cheques to clear through the banking system (this issue is dealt with in Chapter 8).

EXAMPLE

On 31 January 2002, Fiona instructs the solicitor to act in relation to a personal injury claim and pays an advance of £60. On 2 February 2002, the solicitor pays £100 on behalf of Fiona.

CLIENT LEDGER ACCOUNT								
Client: Fiona								
Re: Personal injury								
		Office ledger			*Clients' money ledger*			
Date	Detail	DR	CR	Balance	DR	CR	Balance	
31.1.02	Cash: on account					60	60	

CASH ACCOUNT (extract)								
		Office ledger			*Clients' money ledger*			
Date	Detail	DR	CR	Balance	DR	CR	Balance	
31.1.02	Fiona: on account				60			

If the cheque is drawn on the general client bank account, the following picture emerges:

CLIENT LEDGER ACCOUNT								
Client: Fiona								
Re: Personal injury								
		Office ledger			*Clients' money ledger*			
Date	Detail	DR	CR	Balance	DR	CR	Balance	
31.1.02	Cash: on account					60	60	
2.2.02	Cash: disbursement				100		40 DR	

CASH ACCOUNT (extract)								
		Office ledger			*Clients' money ledger*			
Date	Detail	DR	CR	Balance	DR	CR	Balance	
31.1.02	Fiona: on account				60			
2.2.02	Fiona: disbursement					100		

Note

The DR balance on the client ledger account is a clear indication that the SAR have been breached and solicitors in this position would need to rectify the breach immediately upon discovery, thus:

CLIENT LEDGER ACCOUNT

Client: Fiona

Re: Personal injury

Date	Detail	Office ledger			Clients' money ledger		
		DR	CR	Balance	DR	CR	Balance
31.1.02	Cash: on account					60	60
2.2.02	Cash: disbursement				100		40DR
	Cash: TFR: Rectify breach	40		40		40	0

CASH ACCOUNT (extract)

Date	Detail	Office ledger			Clients' money ledger		
		DR	CR	Balance	DR	CR	Balance
31.1.02	Fiona: on account				60		
2.2.02	Fiona: disbursement					100	
	Fiona: TFR: Rectify breach		40		40		

To prevent such a breach, one of the following actions would be required:

- *Either* the money would have to be paid entirely from the office account:

CLIENT LEDGER ACCOUNT

Client: Fiona

Re: Personal injury

Date	Detail	Office ledger			Clients' money ledger		
		DR	CR	Balance	DR	CR	Balance
31.1.02	Cash: on account					60	60
2.2.02	Cash: disbursement	100		100			60

CASH ACCOUNT (extract)

Date	Detail	Office ledger			Clients' money ledger		
		DR	CR	Balance	DR	CR	Balance
31.1.02	Fiona: on account				60		
2.2.02	Fiona: disbursement		100				

■ *Or*, a transfer from office to client would have to be made to enable a cheque for the amount to be drawn on the client bank account:

CLIENT LEDGER ACCOUNT							
Client: Fiona							
Re: Personal injury							
		Office ledger			Clients' money ledger		
Date	Detail	DR	CR	Balance	DR	CR	Balance
31.1.02	Cash: on account					60	60
2.2.02	Cash: transfer	40		40		40	100
	Cash: disbursement		40	40	100		0

CASH ACCOUNT (extract)							
		Office ledger			Clients' money ledger		
Date	Detail	DR	CR	Balance	DR	CR	Balance
31.1.02	Fiona: on account				60		
2.2.02	Fiona: transfer		40		40		
	Fiona: disbursement					100	

'Bounced' cheques

Rule 22, n (v) warns solicitors about the risks of drawing against an uncleared cheque, ie making a payment out before the payment in has cleared 'for fate' (see Chapter 8). If the client's bank subsequently fails to honour the cheque (that is, the cheque 'bounces'), solicitors will have used other clients' money to make the payment, in which case the solicitors or partners would have to pay into the client bank account their own money to cover any payments made out of the uncleared funds. It is worth noting that r 7(2) makes it clear that 'the duty to remedy breaches [of the SAR] rests not only on the person causing the breach, but also on all the principals in the practice'. In fact, in many cases it is likely that the principals, the partners directors or members, are more likely to be financially able to make the required contribution to correct the deficit of the clients' funds; however, this may not always be the case.

EXAMPLE

A solicitor receives a cheque from Julia on 10 April 2002, for £100 on account of costs and disbursements in relation to a conveyance. On 12 April the solicitor draws a cheque on the client account for £60 to pay a search fee on her behalf. On 14 April, the bank informs the solicitor that it is unable to meet the cheque received from Julia.

First, the cash on account is recorded:

CLIENT LEDGER ACCOUNT							
Client: Julia							
Re: Conveyance							
		Office ledger			Clients' money ledger		
Date	Detail	DR	CR	Balance	DR	CR	Balance
10.4.02	Cash: on account					100	100

CASH ACCOUNT (extract)							
		Office ledger			Clients' money ledger		
Date	Detail	DR	CR	Balance	DR	CR	Balance
10.4.02	Julia: on account				100		

Then the payment of the disbursement on 12 April is recorded:

CLIENT LEDGER ACCOUNT							
Client: Julia							
Re: Conveyance							
		Office ledger			Clients' money ledger		
Date	Detail	DR	CR	Balance	DR	CR	Balance
10.4.02	Cash: on account					100	100
12.4.02	Cash: search fee				60		40

CASH ACCOUNT (extract)							
		Office ledger			Clients' money ledger		
Date	Detail	DR	CR	Balance	DR	CR	Balance
10.4.02	Julia: on account				100		
12.4.02	Julia: search fee					60	

The dishonouring of the cheque requires the initial entries to be reversed:

CLIENT LEDGER ACCOUNT							
Client: Julia							
Re: Conveyance							
		Office ledger			Clients' money ledger		
Date	Detail	DR	CR	Balance	DR	CR	Balance
10.4.02	Cash: on account					100	100
12.4.02	Cash: search fee				60		40
14.4.02	Cash: dishonoured cheque				100		60DR

CASH ACCOUNT (extract)							
		Office ledger			Clients' money ledger		
Date	Detail	DR	CR	Balance	DR	CR	Balance
10.4.02	Julia: on account				100		
12.4.02	Julia: search fee					60	
14.4.02	Julia: dishonoured cheque					100	

The dishonouring of the cheque means that the firm, or partners, upon discovering that the cheque has bounced, will have to transfer from the office bank account to the client bank account, an amount equivalent to that which has been paid out against the uncleared funds.

CLIENT LEDGER ACCOUNT							
Client: Julia							
Re: Conveyance							
		Office ledger			Clients' money ledger		
Date	Detail	DR	CR	Balance	DR	CR	Balance
10.4.02	Cash: on account					100	100
12.4.02	Cash: search fee				60		40
14.4.02	Cash: dishonoured cheque				100		60DR
	Cash: transfer: deficiency	60		60		60	0

CASH ACCOUNT (extract)							
		Office ledger			Clients' money ledger		
Date	Detail	DR	CR	Balance	DR	CR	Balance
10.4.02	Julia: on account				100		
12.4.02	Julia: search fee					60	
14.4.02	Julia: dishonoured cheque					100	
	Julia: transfer: deficiency		60		60		

Note

The transfer required is for the amount paid out not for the amount of the cheque received, unless this has been fully expended.

A similar transfer from office-to-client is required whenever there is discovered a breach of the rules which involves client money having been wrongly paid out.

The most effective safeguard to prevent this situation occurring is for firms to have an internal policy that payments should be made only from cleared funds. Professional Standards Bulletin 16 (para 4.3) suggested that a check should be made to ensure that there are adequate cleared funds before making a payment. (Note that these 'guidelines' are no more than *guidance*, and it is clearly stated that 'they do not override, or detract from the need to comply fully with, the Accounts Rules' (Appendix 3 to the SAR 1998, para 1.1).) Unfortunately, the later guidance in Appendix 3 to the SAR 1998 is weaker than the original Bulletin 16, stating merely that: 'Where payments are to be made other than out of cleared funds, clear policies and procedures must be in place to ensure that adequate risk assessment is applied' (Appendix 3, para 4.3). We consider this to be inadequate protection for clients' money, since solicitors' assessments may be inaccurate. We also consider that this conflicts with r 22(5) which states that: 'money withdrawn in relation to a particular client or controlled trust from a general client account must not exceed the money held on behalf of that client or controlled trust.'

The more commercially aware solicitors also have an internal policy that no disbursements are to be paid out of the office bank account. The combination of these two internal policies effectively requires solicitors to obtain from their clients sufficient cleared funds prior to any payment out. In the long run, this is better for both client and solicitor.

Split money

Rule 20(2) permits alternative treatments for mixed receipts. One option is to split the amount between office and client bank accounts. To split a single cheque, the solicitor, on depositing the cheque, must instruct the bank to credit the office bank account with the office element and the client bank account with the client element. The second option is to pay the entire amount into a client bank account, in which case any office money must be transferred from the office bank account into the client bank account within 14 days of receipt.

EXAMPLE

A solicitor acts for Brenda in a copyright matter. Having completed the work, on 6 May 2002 the solicitor bills Brenda for £600 + VAT, plus anticipated expert's fees of £235. On 13 May 2002, Brenda sends in a cheque for £940, which the solicitor banks, splitting the money between office and client bank accounts. The client ledger account and cash account will appear as:

CLIENT LEDGER ACCOUNT

Client: Brenda

Re: Copyright matter

		Office ledger			Clients' money ledger		
Date	Detail	DR	CR	Balance	DR	CR	Balance
6.5.02	Fees	600					
	VAT	105		705			
13.5.02	Cash: split cheque		705			235	235

CASH ACCOUNT (extract)

		Office ledger			Clients' money ledger		
Date	Detail	DR	CR	Balance	DR	CR	Balance
13.5.02	Brenda: split cheque	705			235		

Splitting the cheque not only involves fewer accounting entries than if the total amount had been paid into the client account with a subsequent transfer out, but also has the cash flow advantage of getting the money into the solicitor's office account as soon as possible. However, for record-keeping purposes and to provide an 'audit trail', it is important that the records clearly show that a single cheque has been split.

EXERCISES

1. After completion of a matter, the client's ledger account shows a debit balance on the office side of the ledger account of £117.50 in relation to a bill of costs delivered and a credit balance of £117.50 on the client account. The solicitor now instructs the bank to transfer £117.50 from the client bank account into the office bank account. What entries will be made on the client ledger account to record the client-to-office transfer? What other entries will have to be made and in which account(s)?

2. A solicitor receives a cheque for £500 from a client on account of costs and disbursements. Before the cheque has cleared, a disbursement of £300 is made from the client bank account. The client's cheque is then dishonoured. What will be the appropriate accounting entries to record the dishonouring of the cheque and its consequences?

3. What steps should a solicitor take to avoid a client's ledger account going overdrawn?

4. What are the consequences if a client ledger account becomes overdrawn?

Chapter 6

Disbursements and VAT

INTRODUCTION

In acting for clients, solicitors frequently make payments for services provided by others. When making payments on behalf of clients, in addition to the regular question of which bank account should be used to make the payment, other questions arise:

■ Should the solicitor add VAT to the payment when recharging (billing) the client?

■ What accounting entries are needed?

■ Who can reclaim the VAT (if any) on the charge for the supply of goods or services to the solicitor by a third party (ie whose VAT is it)?

Expenses incurred on behalf of clients are often referred to as 'disbursements', though common usage is not always a good guide to correct practice.

The term 'disbursements' has a statutory definition: 'costs payable in discharge of a liability properly incurred by . . . [a solicitor] . . . on behalf of the party to be charged' (Solicitors Act 1974, s 67). Rule 2 of the SAR 1998 also provides a definition: 'any sum spent or to be spent on behalf of the client or controlled trust (including any VAT element).'

Examples of disbursements which meet these definitions are: court fees; Land Registry fees; company search fees; annual return fees; stamp duty; local authority search fees and local land charges searches. No VAT is charged on these payments, whether made by the solicitor or by the client. If the solicitor first pays the disbursement from his or her own money, no VAT will be added when the solicitor finally recharges the disbursement to the client.

Other genuine disbursements are: courier charges; photocopying bureau charges; search agents' charges; counsels' fees; and translators' fees, all of which are VATable, unless the solicitor is merely acting as an intermediary or agent (see below).

ACCOUNTING FOR PAID DISBURSEMENTS

In accounting terms, there are two possible methods of treating certain disbursements: solicitors may treat themselves either as principals in the transaction or more simply as agents for their clients.

The principal method

The principal method of accounting requires solicitors to account for the expenses invoiced to them as their own inputs. Any VAT on these is reclaimed by the solicitor. When the cost is recharged to the client, as any other practice expense would be, the solicitor treats the expense (net of VAT) effectively as a profit cost on which VAT would be added and dealt with through the office ledger (though the bill for fees may show the fees and disbursements separately). Using this method, the solicitor reclaims the VAT paid to the provider as input tax and the client is billed for the output VAT on fees plus the expenses.

EXAMPLE

On 9 November 2001, a solicitor, who is holding £1,000 in the general client bank account for a corporate client Werthan Ltd, is invoiced for and pays a photocopying bureau, Faircop & Co, charges of £100 + VAT for copying documentation for a shareholders' circular. Faircop's invoice is addressed to the solicitor. On 23 November, the solicitor bills Werthan Ltd for fees of £300 + VAT and the disbursement.

First, we need to record the payment of Faircop's invoice. The payment must come from the office bank account (even if there are sufficient funds in the client bank account held for this client). Client money should not be used to pay a solicitor's liability. In the ledger account for cash, the VAT will be separately identified because the other side of the double-entry is in the VAT account. The client ledger account is debited with the net of VAT expense.

CLIENT LEDGER ACCOUNT							
Client: Werthan Ltd							
Re: Corporate circular							
		Office ledger			Clients' money ledger		
Date	Detail	DR	CR	Balance	DR	CR	Balance
	Opening balance						1,000
9.11.01	Cash: Faircop	100		100			
	(VAT to be added)						

CASH ACCOUNT (extract)							
		Office ledger			Clients' money ledger		
Date	Detail	DR	CR	Balance	DR	CR	Balance
9.11.01	Werthan Ltd:		100.00				
	Faircop charges						
	VAT		17.50				

VAT ACCOUNT (extract)				
Date	Detail	DR	CR	Balance
9.11.01	Cash: Faircop	17.50		

So the double-entry is:

Debit:	Client ledger account	£100.00
Debit:	VAT account	£ 17.50
Credit:	Cash account	£117.50

When the solicitor bills the client for fees of £300 and disbursement, VAT will be charged on the total of the disbursement and fees, the total value of the services supplied by the solicitor.

CLIENT LEDGER ACCOUNT							
Client: Werthan Ltd							
Re: Corporate circular							
		Office ledger			Clients' money ledger		
Date	Detail	DR	CR	Balance	DR	CR	Balance
	Opening balance						1,000
9.11.01	Cash: Faircop	100		100			
	(VAT to be added)						
23.11.01	Fees	300					
	VAT (on total £400)	70		470			

CASH ACCOUNT (extract)							
		Office ledger			Clients' money ledger		
Date	Detail	DR	CR	Balance	DR	CR	Balance
9.11.01	Werthan Ltd:		100.00				
	Faircop charges						
	VAT		17.50				

VAT ACCOUNT (extract)				
Date	Detail	DR	CR	Balance
9.11.01	Cash: Faircop	17.50		
23.11.01	Werthan Ltd		70.00	

FEES ACCOUNT (extract)				
Date	Detail	DR	CR	Balance
23.11.01	Werthan Ltd		300	

The transfer from the client bank account to the office bank account can now be made for £470.

CLIENT LEDGER ACCOUNT							
Client: Werthan Ltd							
Re: Corporate circular							
		Office ledger			Clients' money ledger		
Date	Detail	DR	CR	Balance	DR	CR	Balance
	Opening balance						1,000
9.11.01	Cash: Faircop	100		100			
	(VAT to be added)						
23.11.01	Fees	300					
	VAT (on total £400)	70		470			
	Cash: TFR: fees + disbursements		470		470		530

CASH ACCOUNT (extract)							
		Office ledger			Clients' money ledger		
Date	Detail	DR	CR	Balance	DR	CR	Balance
9.11.01	Werthan Ltd:		100.00				
	Faircop charges						
	VAT		17.50				
23.11.01	Werthan: TFR: fees + disbursements	470				470	

However, it would have made more sense, from the solicitor's point of view, to transfer the money for the disbursement net of VAT on 9 November, since there is no requirement first to deliver a bill to the client (see r 22, n (l)).

The agency method

An alternative treatment could be adopted if the invoice from Faircop is made out to Werthan Ltd. In this case solicitors may treat themselves as agents in relation to the payment, but only if all the following conditions are met:

the services supplied by the third party are additional to those rendered by solicitors;

clients actually receive the services of the third party;

clients are responsible for paying the third party, ie the third party invoices the client not the solicitor, although the invoice may be sent to the solicitor;

clients know that the third party will supply the services;

clients authorise the solicitor to pay on their behalf;

the expense of the third party supply is separately identified on solicitors' bill for fees; and

solicitors recharge only the exact amount paid to the supplier.

EXAMPLE

If Faircop's invoice is addressed to Werthan Ltd, which has agreed that the solicitor will act as its agent in paying the invoice (and all the other necessary conditions have been met), then the entries under the agency basis would be:

CLIENT LEDGER ACCOUNT							
Client: Werthan Ltd							
Re: Corporate matter							
		Office ledger			Clients' money ledger		
Date	Detail	DR	CR	Balance	DR	CR	Balance
	Opening balance						1,000
9.11.01	Cash: Faircop	117.50		117.50			

CASH ACCOUNT (extract)							
		Office ledger			Clients' money ledger		
Date	Detail	DR	CR	Balance	DR	CR	Balance
9.11.01	Werthan Ltd: Faircop charges		117.50				

Now the bill is delivered:

CLIENT LEDGER ACCOUNT							
Client: Werthan Ltd							
Re: Corporate matter							
		Office ledger			*Clients' money ledger*		
Date	Detail	DR	CR	Balance	DR	CR	Balance
	Opening balance						1,000
9.11.01	Cash: Faircop	117.50		117.50			

CASH ACCOUNT (extract)							
		Office ledger			*Clients' money ledger*		
Date	Detail	DR	CR	Balance	DR	CR	Balance
9.11.01	Werthan Ltd:		117.50				
	Faircop charges						

VAT ACCOUNT (extract)				
Date	Detail	DR	CR	Balance
23.11.01	Werthan Ltd		52.50	

FEES ACCOUNT (extract)				
Date	Detail	DR	CR	Balance
23.11.01	Werthan Ltd		300	

Then the client-to-office transfer is made:

CASH ACCOUNT (extract)							
		Office ledger			*Clients' money ledger*		
Date	Detail	DR	CR	Balance	DR	CR	Balance
9.11.01	Werthan Ltd:		117.50				
	Faircop charges						
23.11.01	Werthan Ltd:	470.00				470.00	
	TFR: Fees + disbursements						

Better still, from the point of view of the solicitors, is to use the client bank account to make the payment, provided of course that sufficient cleared funds are held for that client. Thus:

CLIENT LEDGER ACCOUNT							
Client: Werthan Ltd							
Re: Corporate matter							
		Office ledger			Clients' money ledger		
Date	Detail	DR	CR	Balance	DR	CR	Balance
	Balance						1,000.00
9.11.01	Cash: Faircop				117.50		882.50

CASH ACCOUNT (extract)							
		Office ledger			Clients' money ledger		
Date	Detail	DR	CR	Balance	DR	CR	Balance
9.11.01	Werthan Ltd:					117.50	
	Faircop charges						

The billing to the client will appear on the client ledger account as follows (the fees and VAT accounts are the same as before):

CLIENT LEDGER ACCOUNT							
Client: Werthan Ltd							
Re: Corporate matter							
		Office ledger			Clients' money ledger		
Date	Detail	DR	CR	Balance	DR	CR	Balance
	Balance						1,000.00
9.11.01	Cash: Faircop				117.50		882.50
23.11.01	Fees	300.00					
	VAT	52.50		352.50			

After the transfer from client bank account to office bank account has been made:

CLIENT LEDGER ACCOUNT							
Client: Werthan Ltd							
Re: Corporate matter							
		Office ledger			Clients' money ledger		
Date	Detail	DR	CR	Balance	DR	CR	Balance
	Balance						1,000.00
9.11.01	Cash: Faircop				117.50		882.50
23.11.01	Fees	300.00					
	VAT	52.50		352.50			
	Cash: TFR: fees + disbursements		352.50		352.50		530.00

Note

It makes no difference which method is used, the client will be billed and will pay the same total sum, £470.

VAT status of client and supplier

Solicitors need to be aware of the VAT position in regard to payments for their clients. Ignorance may cause unnecessary expense to the client.

It makes no real difference (apart from cash flow advantages) to a VAT-registered client which method (principal or agent) is used because whatever VAT the solicitor charges can be recovered, provided it is a business matter. Similarly, when the client is not VAT-registered but the third party supplier is VAT-registered, the client will end up paying the same total, regardless of whether the principal or agency method is used.

However, the choice of method may make a difference when *neither* the photocopying bureau *nor* the client is VAT-registered. If Faircop is not VAT-registered, then there will be no VAT on its invoice but there will be VAT added to the solicitor's recharge to Werthan Ltd. If the agency method is used, the solicitor is acting only as intermediary, and will not have to add VAT to the disbursement. It is therefore better, whenever possible, for solicitors to arrange to act as the client's agent.

EXAMPLE

CLIENT LEDGER ACCOUNT

Client: Werthan Ltd

Re: Corporate circular

		Office ledger			Clients' money ledger		
Date	Detail	DR	CR	Balance	DR	CR	Balance
	Opening balance						1,000
9.11.01	Cash: Faircop	100.00		100.00			1,000
23.11.01	Fees	300.00					1,000
	VAT (on fees only)	52.50		452.50			

CASH ACCOUNT (extract)

		Office ledger			Clients' money ledger		
Date	Detail	DR	CR	Balance	DR	CR	Balance
9.11.01	Werthan Ltd: Faircop charges		100				

VAT ACCOUNT (extract)

Date	Detail	DR	CR	Balance
23.11.01	Werthan Ltd		52.50	

FEES ACCOUNT (extract)

Date	Detail	DR	CR	Balance
23.11.01	Werthan Ltd		300	

However, if the agency conditions are not met and the principal method has to be used, then the solicitor will have to add VAT to the full value of the service, even though no VAT was charged by Faircop. The addition of VAT on the bureau's costs will increase the expense to the client by an amount which cannot be recovered by the non-VAT-registered client.

CLIENT LEDGER ACCOUNT

Client: Werthan Ltd

Re: Corporate circular

		Office ledger			Clients' money ledger		
Date	Detail	DR	CR	Balance	DR	CR	Balance
	Opening balance						1,000
9.11.01	Cash: Faircop	100		100			
	(VAT to be added)						
23.11.01	Fees	300					
	VAT (on total £400)	70		470			

CASH ACCOUNT (extract)

		Office ledger			Clients' money ledger		
Date	Detail	DR	CR	Balance	DR	CR	Balance
9.11.01	Werthan Ltd:		100				
	Faircop charges						

VAT ACCOUNT (extract)

Date	Detail	DR	CR	Balance
23.11.01	Werthan Ltd		70	

FEES ACCOUNT (extract)

Date	Detail	DR	CR	Balance
23.11.01	Werthan Ltd		300	

Note that the solicitor is unaffected by the choice of treatment; it is the client's interests which are affected. However, solicitors who apply the wrong treatment are likely to find themselves in trouble with the Customs and Excise authorities. For instance, some expenses for services supplied directly to and paid for by solicitors may not carry VAT, for example, postage, bank transfer charges, rail fares. These may be referred to as 'disbursements' in practice but are more correctly known as 'overheads', 'sundry charges', or 'incidental expenses', since they are incurred in order to enable solicitors to provide services to the client. Other examples of such overheads include: office photocopies; telephone calls; fax charges; secretarial overtime; and Lexis charges. These indirect expenses are VATable regardless of whether any VAT was charged to the solicitor: they are part of the value of the services provided by solicitors. These expenses can be distinguished from true disbursements because when they are incurred they are the liability of the solicitor not the client: they are not ordered directly by the client, nor has the client agreed that the solicitor should incur them but, more importantly, they are services to the solicitor to enable him or her to carry out their professional functions. These indirect costs should be recovered as part of solicitors' fees and VAT should be added to solicitors' bills even though they may have paid no VAT on the expense. Essentially, these expenses fail to meet the agency conditions.

Although solicitors have contested the Customs and Excise treatment, Customs have always succeeded in obtaining rulings to support their views, the outcome of which is that VAT is chargeable by the solicitor on all indirect expenses and on some (but not all) genuine disbursements.

A recent case illustrates the strict legal position. In *Shuttleworth & Co* (LON/94/986) Simon's Weekly Tax Intelligence, 198, a firm claimed that the charge for a bank transfer was a disbursement (and therefore not liable to VAT, since no VAT is charged by the bank to the solicitor because the transfer of money is an exempt supply of finance). Customs and Excise successfully argued that the bank's services were supplied to the firm not to the firm's client, the transfer was part of the services rendered by the firm to its client and must be liable to VAT. This is consistent with the finding in *Rowe & Maw v C & E* (1975) 1 BVC 51. The Law Society's *Gazette* reports that the Society has always agreed with Customs' view that such services are VATable (see *Gazette* 21 February 1990, p 14; 18 November 1992, p 41; and 1 March 1995, p 30).

The effect of the VAT point

Complications can arise when the supplier's invoice is received on one day, the client is billed on another and the respective debts are settled on different days.

Principal method

EXAMPLE

Assume now that the solicitor acting for Werthan Ltd holds no money in the client bank account on behalf of Werthan and has been instructed to act as principal in employing the services of Faircop. The following events then occur:

9 November	Faircop delivers the copies and invoices the solicitor for £100 plus VAT;
23 November	the solicitor then delivers a bill for fees of £300 + £100 disbursements + VAT (on the total);
28 November	the solicitor pays the bureau £100 plus VAT;
30 November	the solicitor receives payment from the client for the full amount billed.

CLIENT LEDGER ACCOUNT							
Client: Werthan Ltd							
Re: Corporate matter							
		Office ledger			*Clients' money ledger*		
Date	Detail	DR	CR	Balance	DR	CR	Balance
9.11.01	Faircop: copies (VAT to be added)	100		100			

VAT ACCOUNT (extract)				
Date	Detail	DR	CR	Balance
9.11.01	Faircop: Werthan Ltd	17.50		

FAIRCOP SUPPLIER'S ACCOUNT				
Date	Detail	DR	CR	Balance
9.11.01	Werthan Ltd		100.00	
	VAT		17.50	

Note

When Faircop's invoice is received, this creates a liability of the solicitor (under the accruals concept). The VAT is debited to the VAT account unless the solicitor is on the cash accounting scheme (ie accounting for VAT on payments and receipts of money as opposed to reclaiming VAT on the invoices for goods and services received from suppliers and accounting to Customs for VAT on bills delivered).

Now the solicitor charges the client:

CLIENT LEDGER ACCOUNT							
Client: Werthan Ltd							
Re: Corporate matter							
		Office ledger			Clients' money ledger		
Date	Detail	DR	CR	Balance	DR	CR	Balance
9.11.01	Faircop: copies	100		100			
23.11.01	Fees	300					
	VAT	70		470			

VAT ACCOUNT (extract)				
Date	Detail	DR	CR	Balance
9.11.01	Faircop: Werthan Ltd	17.50		
23.11.01	Werthan: fees		70.00	

FAIRCOP SUPPLIER'S ACCOUNT				
Date	Detail	DR	CR	Balance
9.11.01	Werthan Ltd		100.00	
	VAT		17.50	

FEES ACCOUNT (extract)

Date	Detail	DR	CR	Balance
23.11.01	Werthan Ltd		300	

When payment is made to the bureau it must be from the office bank account, since the solicitor is acting as principal. It would be a breach of the rules to use client money to pay a liability of the solicitor.

When the client pays, this is office money.

CLIENT LEDGER ACCOUNT

Client: Werthan Ltd

Re: Corporate matter

		Office ledger			Clients' money ledger		
Date	Detail	DR	CR	Balance	DR	CR	Balance
9.11.01	Faircop: copies	100		100			
23.11.01	Fees	300					
	VAT	70		470			
30.11.01	Cash		470	0			

CASH ACCOUNT (extract)

		Office ledger			Clients' money ledger		
Date	Detail	DR	CR	Balance	DR	CR	Balance
28.11.01	Faircop: re Werthan		117.50				
30.11.01	Werthan	470.00					

VAT ACCOUNT (extract)

Date	Detail	DR	CR	Balance
9.11.01	Faircop: Werthan Ltd	17.50		
23.11.01	Werthan: fees		70.00	

FAIRCOP SUPPLIER'S ACCOUNT

Date	Detail	DR	CR	Balance
9.11.01	Werthan Ltd		100.00	
	VAT		17.50	117.50
28.11.01	Cash	117.50		0.00

FEES ACCOUNT (extract)				
Date	Detail	DR	CR	Balance
23.11.01	Werthan Ltd		300	

Where the solicitor is holding sufficient funds for this client in the client bank account, the payment must still first come from office with a subsequent client-to-office transfer being made.

CLIENT LEDGER ACCOUNT							
Client: Werthan Ltd							
Re: Corporate matter							
		Office ledger			*Clients' money ledger*		
Date	Detail	DR	CR	Balance	DR	CR	Balance
	Opening balance						1,000
9.11.01	Faircop: copies	100		100			
23.11.01	Fees	300					
	VAT	70		470			
30.11.01	Cash: TFR: fees and disbursements		470		470		530

CASH ACCOUNT (extract)							
		Office ledger			*Clients' money ledger*		
Date	Detail	DR	CR	Balance	DR	CR	Balance
28.11.01	Faircop: re Werthan		117.50				
30.11.01	Werthan: TFR: fees and disbursements	470				470	

The agency method

Under this method the supply is deemed to be direct to the client, who can then reclaim the input VAT (if registered) and no VAT entries need to be made in the solicitor's books.

EXAMPLE

Taking the same example as before, but now the solicitor treats the bureau's fee on the agency basis:

CLIENT LEDGER ACCOUNT							
Client: Werthan Ltd							
Re: Corporate matter							
		Office ledger			Clients' money ledger		
Date	Detail	DR	CR	Balance	DR	CR	Balance
23.11.01	Fees	300.00					
	VAT	52.50		352.50			
28.11.01	Cash: Faircop	117.50		470.00			
30.11.01	Cash: from you		470.00	0.00			

CASH ACCOUNT (extract)							
		Office ledger			Clients' money ledger		
Date	Detail	DR	CR	Balance	DR	CR	Balance
28.11.01	Faircop: Werthan Ltd		117.50				
30.11.01	Werthan Ltd: Fees + disbursements	470.00					

VAT ACCOUNT (extract)				
Date	Detail	DR	CR	Balance
23.11.01	Werthan Ltd		52.50	

FEES ACCOUNT (extract)				
Date	Detail	DR	CR	Balance
23.11.01	Werthan Ltd		300	

Note

(i) The bill for fees from the solicitor will include the total due in respect of the bureau's bill including VAT:

	£
Own fees	300.00
Add VAT at 17½%	52.50
	352.50
Add photocopying cost	117.50
	470.00

(ii) No VAT entries are made in the solicitor's books in regard to the photocopying bureau's invoice.

(iii) The receipt of money from the client will be paid into the office bank account.

EXERCISES

1. What conditions must be met before solicitors can treat themselves as agents rather than principals in making a disbursement or payment for a client?

2. What difference does it make to the client whether the solicitor acts as agent or principal?

3. Give examples of disbursements which are VATable and those which are not VATable.

4. From which bank account must the payment be made if the solicitor is acting as (a) agent, or (b) principal?

5. What are the entries to record the payment of a disbursement of £200 + £35 VAT if the solicitor is acting as (a) agent, or (b) principal?

Chapter 7

Trust money

INTRODUCTION

For the purposes of the SAR 1998, money subject to a trust will be either:

- controlled trust money; or
- client money, when the trust is not a controlled trust (r 13, n (vii)).

Solicitors who act as trustees in conjunction with another person or persons outside the firm, for example a member of the client's family, are subject to the general requirements of all trustees: in particular, they are required to keep proper accounting records to show how they have handled the money of the trust and they must not benefit from their position as trustees.

WHAT IS A CONTROLLED TRUST?

According to r 2, a controlled trust arises when:

- a solicitor acts as the sole trustee or co-trustee only with one or more of their partners or employees;
- a solicitor who is a director or employee of a recognised body is the sole trustee of a trust, or co-trustee only with one or more of the recognised body's other officers or employees or with the recognised body itself;
- a registered foreign lawyer who is a partner in a multinational partnership is, by dint of being a partner in that partnership, the sole trustee of a trust, or co-trustee only with one or more of the other partners or employees;
- a registered foreign lawyer who is the director of a recognised body is, by dint of practising as a director of the recognised body, the sole trustee of a trust, or co-trustee only with one or more of the recognised body's other officers or employees or with the recognised body itself; or
- a recognised body is the sole trustee of a trust, or co-trustee only with one or more of the recognised body's officers, members or employees.

Relevant definitions

- A 'controlled trustee' is a trustee of a controlled trust.

- A 'multinational partnership' is a partnership comprising one or more solicitors and one or more registered foreign lawyers.

- A 'recognised body' means a company or LLP recognised by the Society under s 9 of the Administration of Justice Act 1985.

- A 'registered foreign lawyer' refers to a person registered by the Society under s 89 of the Courts and Legal Services Act 1990.

- A 'trustee' includes a personal representative (that is, an executor or an administrator).

Note that although controlled trust money is not 'clients' money' (r 13), it must be paid into a client bank account (r 15(1)), subject to certain exceptions. The definition of a client [bank] account is one in which client money and/or controlled trust money is held (r 13(2)). The purpose of this broad definition is to simplify the rules so that, in most contexts, the same rules apply to client money and to controlled trust money. Controlled trust money may be held either in a separate current or deposit account including in its title a reference to the identity of the controlled trust or in a general client bank account (r 14(5)). For practical reasons relating to accounting for interest, it is preferable to keep the money for each controlled trust in a separate designated bank account (see Chapter 8).

As with clients' money generally (see Chapter 3), under r 15(2) solicitors may pay into a client bank account money other than that which is subject to the trust if it is:

- the solicitor's own money required to open or maintain the bank account;

- an advance from the solicitor to fund a payment in excess of the funds held for that controlled trust;

- money to replace any sum withdrawn in breach of r 22 (see below); or

- a sum in lieu of interest to be paid to the beneficiaries of the trust (although see below).

Solicitors may also pay into a client bank account money received in full or part settlement of their bill (r 19(1)(c)) provided any office money is transferred out within 14 days of receipt.

Rule 20 deals with 'mixed payments', ie receipts which include both client or controlled trust money as well as office money. A mixed payment may either be split into its constituent parts (client/controlled trust money and office money) or paid *in toto* into a client bank account, in which case all office money must be transferred out within 14 days of receipt.

Solicitors are not required to pay into a client bank account controlled trust money which is:

- received in cash and is without delay paid in the execution of the trust to a beneficiary or third party;

- a cheque or draft received and without delay endorsed over in the execution of the trust to a beneficiary or third party;

- kept in some other type of bank account (in accordance with the trustee's powers) or is properly held in the form of cash; or

- withheld on the written authorisation of the Law Society.

A withdrawal of controlled trust money is permitted by r 22(2) only when it is:

  money properly required for a payment in the execution of the particular trust, including the purchase of an investment within the trustee's powers;

  money required for a disbursement for the trust;

  money to reimburse solicitors for payments from their own money on behalf of the trust;

  money to be transferred to another client bank account or another type of bank account if the trustee's powers allow, or to be properly retained in cash in the performance of the trustees duties;

  to reimburse solicitors for an advance no longer required;

  money paid into the bank account in breach of the rules; or

  money withdrawn on the written authorisation of the Law Society.

Before solicitors can withdraw their fees from money held in a client bank account, they must first send a bill to the paying party – here the controlled trustees – and the solicitors themselves; and the required records need to be kept (r 19, n (xi)), ie a copy of the original bill on a central record or file as required by r 32(8). Once this has been done and the work completed (n (ix)) the money earmarked for costs (ie fees plus disbursements) becomes office money and must be transferred out of the client bank account within 14 days (r 19(3)).

Accounting records

Solicitors must keep proper accounting records to show their dealings with:

  controlled trust money received, held or paid including that which is not held in a client bank account (r 32(1)(b)); and

  any office money relating to any controlled trust matter (r 32(1)(c));

A solicitor is required to keep separate ledger accounts for each controlled trust (r 32(2)(b)).

Controlled trust money held in a passbook-operated separate designated bank account is subject to the reconciliation procedure every 14 weeks; in all other cases the reconciliation must be performed every five weeks.

Statements and passbooks for controlled trust money held outside a client bank account must be kept (r 32(9)(b)(iv)) and must be held together centrally or in a central register of these accounts (r 32(11)).

Chapter 8

Accounting to the client for interest

BACKGROUND

Historically, solicitors have retained for themselves any interest earned on clients' money. They felt able to do this because the early SAR were silent as to whether there was any obligation to pay interest to clients. However, following the decision in *Brown v IRC* [1964] 3 All ER 119, HL, s 8 of the Solicitors Act 1965 required the Law Society to make rules prescribing the treatment of interest arising on clients' funds. The Solicitors' Accounts (Deposit Interest) Rules 1965 were the first to be enacted.

The current Rules are found in Part C of the SAR (rr 24-28) and are made under s 33 of the Solicitors Act 1974, as amended by s 125(7) of the Courts and Legal Services Act 1990.

The Monitoring and Investigation Unit of the Office for the Supervision of Solicitors (OSS) finds that solicitors are frequently in breach of this aspect of the rules, either because they do not pay any interest at all or because they pay an inadequate amount.

GENERAL AND DESIGNATED CLIENT ACCOUNTS

There are two types of client bank account:

■ general client bank accounts; and
■ separate designated client bank accounts.

Solicitors must open the latter type if so instructed by their clients but may do so in other circumstances. However, it is not only common but also sensible practice for solicitors to hold most of their clients' money in a general client bank account. Indeed, some solicitors have general client bank accounts with several banks (or building societies) for various commercial reasons.

ENTITLEMENT TO INTEREST

Interest earned on a separate designated bank account belongs to the client, and solicitors must account for all the interest on such bank accounts (r 24(1)). It is important to remember that the 'de minimis' provision mentioned later in this chapter does not apply to interest earned on separate designated bank accounts.

Solicitors are entitled to retain bank interest earned on clients' money placed in a general client bank account (Solicitors Act 1974, s 33(3)). Since interest earned on moneys in a general client bank account belongs to solicitors, it must be paid direct into their office or personal bank account. If the bank wrongly credits such interest to the firm's general client bank account, it must be removed immediately (r 22(3)).

However, this general principle is subject to the obligation imposed on solicitors by r 24(2) to pay clients from their own money a sum in lieu of interest unless exempt under r 24(3). The general intention (although this is not stated explicitly) is that clients are to be placed in the same position whether their money is banked in a separate designated bank account or in the firm's general client bank account.

PAYMENTS IN LIEU OF INTEREST

When do solicitors have to pay their clients a sum in lieu of interest? The r 24(3) table sets out the circumstances in which solicitors are *not* required to make a payment in lieu by reference to minimum amounts of money and minimum periods of time for which such amounts are held.

The Rule 24 Table

Amount	Time
£1,000	8 weeks
£2,000	4 weeks
£10,000	2 weeks
£20,000	1 week

We think that the rule is easier to understand if it is expressed positively rather than in the negative. Thus, our interpretation of r 24 is that solicitors must make a payment in lieu of interest if:

- they have held more than £1,000 for more than eight weeks;
- they have held more than £2,000 for more than four weeks;
- they have held more than £10,000 for more than two weeks; or
- they have held more than £20,000 for more than one week.

If more than £20,000 is held for one week or less, solicitors are required to make a payment in lieu of interest when it is fair and reasonable to do so.

Calculation of interest

The calculation of interest follows this formula:

Amount x interest rate x period held

The period for which the money is held is expressed as a fraction of the year, since interest rates are invariably quoted as rates per annum.

EXAMPLE

A solicitor acts on behalf of Crystal in connection with the sale of a property. On 6 January 2002, the solicitor receives the sale proceeds of £21,000. The money is received by telegraphic transfer (TT) into the general client bank account, where it remains until 19 January 2002, when the solicitor makes a TT to Crystal. The solicitor must make a calculation of the payment in lieu of interest since the table applies when more than £20,000 has been held for more than a week. Assuming a rate of interest of 3% per annum, the calculation is:

£21,000 x 3/100 x 13/365 = £22.44

The £20 'de minimis'

Even though an amount held in the general client bank account is within the provisions of the table, where the calculation produces a figure of £20 or less, no payment in lieu needs to be made (r 24(3)(a)).

Thus, if £21,000 is held for only 11 days, the calculation is:

£21,000 x 3/100 x 11/365 = £18.99

and no payment is due.

As previously stated, if more than £20,000 is held for a week or less, solicitors will have to account for a sum in lieu if this is fair and reasonable (r 24(3)(b)(ii)). We consider that clients could justifiably claim that it is fair and reasonable to receive a sum in lieu whenever this is more than £20. For example, if £21,000 is held for six days and the prevailing interest rate is 6%, the calculation is:

£21,000 x 6/100 x 6/365 = £20.71

Other exceptions

In addition to the £20 'de minimis', solicitors need not make a payment in lieu where:

■ money is held to pay counsel's fees and counsel has requested a delay in settlement;

■ money is held for the Legal Services Commission;

■ the solicitor has advanced money to the client under r 15(2)(b) in order to finance a payment in excess of the funds held for that client; or

■ there is an agreement to contract out of the interest provisions (r 27).

What rate of interest is payable?

The implied aim of Part C of the SAR is to put the client in the same position regardless of whether the money has been paid into a separate designated client bank account or a general client bank account (r 25(1)).

Each client must be looked at individually, since the rate of interest paid on designated accounts may well vary with the bank and amount involved. It may also be different from the rate which the solicitor actually receives on general client bank account funds.

Rule 27(1) permits solicitors to agree with clients terms which vary from the Part C rules, provided this is evidenced in writing by the client. However, it is unlikely that getting clients to agree that they are entitled to no interest will be acceptable. Note (i) to r 27 states that contracting out is never appropriate if it is against the client's interests.

The simplest solution for solicitors is to have terms of business with each client which specify the rate of interest, preferably linked to base rate, provided this does not place the client in a worse position than under the provisions of r 24(2) and r 25(2). It is also a good idea to incorporate the 'de minimis' figure.

An example of such a term is as follows:

> 'The Solicitors' Accounts Rules require us, in certain circumstances, to pay you money in lieu of interest on funds held on your behalf in our general client bank account, if the sum exceeds £20. Where these Rules are applicable, a payment in lieu of interest will be paid to you at the rate of [ ]% below the base rate at [name of bank]. This interest will be paid to you *gross* (ie without any deduction of tax). This may well be a considerable advantage to you. Please note that it will be your responsibility, in such circumstances, to account to the Inland Revenue for tax (if any) due on this money.'

The question of what interest the money could have earned if it had been placed in a separate designated bank account is complicated by several factors.

Tax on interest

Interest on a general client bank account is paid gross, ie without deduction of tax at source, whereas interest on separate designated accounts is usually paid net of tax. Any payment under r 24(2) by the solicitor to the client in lieu of interest must be at a gross rate with the client accounting to the Inland Revenue for any tax due. Prudent solicitors will point this out to their clients. Clients may prefer to receive a gross payment in lieu of interest, as opposed to a net payment of interest arising on a separate designated bank account, either because they are not taxpayers or they, quite sensibly, prefer the cash flow benefit of receiving the gross payment now while paying the relevant tax later.

The solicitor may also prefer to keep client money in a general client bank account as opposed to separate designated accounts. This is because a solicitor with a large balance in a general client bank account will be able to negotiate a higher rate of interest with the bank and the benefit of this can be shared with clients.

Variable balances

The calculation becomes more complex where the balances held for an individual client in a client bank account vary from time to time. Rule 25(2) requires solicitors to calculate the payment in lieu of interest 'on the balance or balances held over the whole period for which cleared funds are held'. This will require a separate sub-calculation each time the balance changes. In manual accounting systems the calculation can be time-consuming, although computerised systems frequently make the calculation instantly.

Clients' money held in general client accounts in several banks or building societies

The solicitor must use the highest rate of interest on offer at any of these institutions for the sum in question from the date it was first paid into the general client bank account (r 25(3)).

Clearance times

For the purposes of calculating the number of weeks in the table, the relevant period should be that for which cleared funds are held (r 25(2)). However, as discussed below, n (iii) to r 25 indicates that this may not always be the case.

There are two types of clearance and it is extremely important to understand the difference between them:

- 'clearance for interest', sometimes referred to as 'clearance for value'; and
- 'clearance for fate', or 'clearance for drawing against'.

Clearance for interest

This is the number of days which must elapse, according to the collecting bank's rules, before interest will start to accrue. Different banks give value according to different cycles; some offer two *working* days, while others require three or four. This means that if a cheque is paid into a general client bank account on a Friday, interest may not be allowed until the Tuesday or Wednesday of the following week, Saturday and Sunday being counted as non-working days. The period of clearance may also vary with the location of the bank on which the cheque is drawn. For example, cheques drawn on Scottish banks and paid into an English bank account may take longer to clear than cheques drawn on other English banks. Of course, money received in the form of cash or by TT is treated as cleared for interest on the day of receipt and will earn interest from that day.

Clearance for fate

This is the period of time which must elapse before it is safe to draw against a cheque which has been paid into a bank account. A solicitor may have to wait between seven and ten working days before being certain that it is safe to draw against a cheque. In practice, banks often allow solicitors to draw against building society cheques immediately they are paid into the bank account because they know that it is unlikely (though not impossible) that the building society cheque will not be honoured. In fact, one of the leading High Street banks has recently started to apply this to any cheque paid in. This presents a trap to the unwary solicitor, who transfers money out of the client bank account by TT the same day that a cheque is paid in, because the solicitor loses interest on the funds transferred out and only starts to gain interest once the cheque paid in has cleared (for interest purposes). The amount of 'lost' interest can be significant over the course of a year if this imprudent practice is carried out regularly. Furthermore, solicitors expose themselves to the risk that the incoming cheque may be stopped, in which case they will have used other clients' money in breach of the SAR and they must rectify the situation immediately upon discovery by transferring their own money into the client bank account (see Chapter 5).

In fact, technically, it will always be a breach of the SAR to pay out against an uncleared cheque because other clients' money will have been used, albeit temporarily. For this reason, we believe that the SAR are contradictory. One of the r 1 principles is that solicitors must use each client's money only for that client's matters and r 22(5) states that money withdrawn on behalf of a client must not exceed money held for that client; yet r 22, n (v) allows solicitors to draw against an uncleared cheque, provided they use their discretion. Equally weak is the guidance in Appendix 3 to the SAR, *Law Society Guidelines – Accounting Procedures and Systems*, para 4.3, which states that, 'where payments are to be made other than out of cleared funds, clear policies and procedures must be in place to ensure that adequate risk assessment is applied'. The problem is that there is always a risk that the incoming cheque will not be met. Even mortgage cheques from institutional lenders can be stopped if the lender obtains new information at the last minute, for example, the death of one of the borrowers or circumstances suggesting mortgage fraud.

To minimise the problems caused by clearance for both interest and fate, solicitors often cover the matter in their terms of business, for example:

> 'We cannot pay out money on your behalf until we are in possession of *cleared funds*. Any cheques must therefore be received by us at least *seven* working days before the money is due to be paid out. If a longer clearance period is required, we shall advise you nearer the date.
>
> Similarly, if we receive cheques for you, they have to be cleared through our bank before we can pay you.'

Wise solicitors have an in-house rule that no payments out are to be made other than out of funds cleared for both interest and fate.

Special clearance

Banks offer a facility, known as 'special clearance', by which they can clear cheques more quickly. However, several factors need to be borne in mind:

- the type of clearance referred to is clearance for fate not clearance for interest;

- there is thus no point in requesting special clearance for institutional cheques which the solicitor has no reason to suspect will not be honoured – for example, a mortgage advance from a building society;

- interest will not begin to accrue until the end of the normal clearance period, even if special clearance is obtained (the main type of cheque for which it is worth requesting special clearance is a cheque from a client which is required to complete a matter but which is received late; even in this event, astute solicitors will request the client to pay them by TT); and

- banks charge for special clearance (the normal fee at present is £15-£20 and it would be sensible for solicitors to obtain their clients' agreement to reimburse this fee).

Payments in lieu

A solicitor will need to be aware of the collecting bank's policy on 'clearance for interest' and should also clarify the position regarding interest on money which is not held for a complete day; for example, will interest be paid on cleared funds on the day of receipt and on the day of payment out or only on one of these days or on neither day? In order to comply with r 25(2), solicitors should consider their banks' period for 'clearance for interest' when calculating payments in lieu of interest. In working out the calculation of interest, we follow a common banking practice, which includes the day cleared funds are received but does not include the day cleared funds are paid out.

However, n (ii) to r 25 states, somewhat optimistically, that, where receipt of money and payment of money are both by cheque, the normal clearance periods will usually cancel each other out, so that the actual clearance times need not be checked.

Different considerations apply when receipt and payment are by different methods. Note (iii) to r 25 states that the relevant period is:

- from the date cash is received to the date the outgoing cheque is *sent*;
- from the date the incoming TT begins to earn interest to the date the outgoing cheque is *sent*;
- from the date when the incoming cheque or bankers' draft is or would normally be cleared until the outgoing TT is made or bankers' draft is obtained.

We seriously doubt whether the first and second of the above treatments produce a result which is fair to the client. This is an example of a conflict between the Rule and the Notes because, as mentioned above, r 25(2) states that the sum in lieu of interest must be calculated over the *whole period for which cleared funds are held*. If, following, n (iii), we end the calculation on the date the outgoing cheque is *sent*, we will be depriving clients of interest to which they may well be entitled. After all, the solicitor will receive interest on the funds until the cheque clears.

Having said this, we accept that it would be unduly onerous to require solicitors to determine the exact date when each individual cheque actually cleared. We feel, however, that a fairer result would have been achieved if solicitors had been required to make a standard allowance for clearance of, say, three days (one day for the mail, and two days for clearance through the banking system). Of course, a client who fails promptly to bank a cheque from the solicitor may claim to be owed a larger sum in lieu of interest. Whether it is reasonable to recalculate the amount due will depend on all the circumstances, and a solicitor may be entitled to charge for this extra work (r 24, n (vii)).

We have devoted some time to the issue of clearance because we know that this is an area which many practising solicitors fail to understand and because the SAR are not sufficiently clear.

Accounting for interest

In the first example of Crystal, above, where £21,000 was held for 13 days and 3% was the relevant interest rate, £22.44 is the sum equivalent to the interest which would have been earned in a separate designated bank account. How is this sum to be paid to Crystal?

EXAMPLE

The direct method

The simplest way is to write an office account cheque to the client for which the accounting entries are:

CASH ACCOUNT (extract)							
		Office Ledger			Clients' Money Ledger		
Date	Detail	DR	CR	Balance	DR	CR	Balance
19.1.02	Interest paid:						
	Crystal		22.44				

INTEREST PAID ACCOUNT (extract)				
Date	Detail	DR	CR	Balance
19.1.02	Cash: Crystal	22.44		

Note

There are no entries in the client ledger account. If the client is also to be paid the £21,000 balance held, a separate cheque would need to be drawn on a client bank account. The interest paid account is an office-only account. It records all payments of interest to clients and others (eg payments of interest to the solicitor's bank on the firm's overdraft). At the end of the year, the balance on this account will be treated as an expense in the firm's profit and loss account.

EXAMPLE

The indirect method

An alternative method of accounting to the client involves a transfer of money from the office bank account into the client bank account, with a subsequent payment out of the client bank account. A sum in lieu of interest is now expressly permitted by r 15(2)(d) to be paid into the client bank account. This method has the advantage of making an entry on the client ledger account which is a permanent record of the payment to the client and may be more convenient for the client who receives only one cheque from the solicitor comprising both the balance and the payment in lieu of interest.

CLIENT LEDGER ACCOUNT							
Client: Crystal							
Re: Sale of property							
		Office Ledger			Clients' Money Ledger		
Date	Detail	DR	CR	Balance	DR	CR	Balance
6.1.02	Balance						21,000.00
19.1.02	Cash: TFR:						
	Interest paid					22.44	21,022.44

CASH ACCOUNT (extract)						
		Office Ledger			*Clients' Money Ledger*	
Date	Detail	DR	CR	Balance	DR	CR	Balance
19.1.02	Interest paid:						
	TFR: Crystal		22.44		22.44		

INTEREST PAID ACCOUNT (extract)				
Date	Detail	DR	CR	Balance
19.1.02	Cash: Crystal	22.44		

Then the entire amount is paid in a single cheque to the client:

CLIENT LEDGER ACCOUNT							
Client: Crystal							
Re: Sale of property							
		Office Ledger			*Clients' Money Ledger*		
Date	Detail	DR	CR	Balance	DR	CR	Balance
6.1.02	Balance						21,000.00
19.1.02	Cash: TFR:						
	Interest paid					22.44	21,022.44
	Cash: balance to you				21,022.44		0.00

CASH ACCOUNT (extract)							
		Office Ledger			*Clients' Money Ledger*		
Date	Detail	DR	CR	Balance	DR	CR	Balance
19.1.02	Interest paid:						
	TFR: Crystal		22.44		22.44		
	Crystal: balance due					21,022.44	

INTEREST PAID ACCOUNT (extract)				
Date	Detail	DR	CR	Balance
19.1.02	Cash: Crystal	22.44		

INTEREST ON STAKEHOLDER MONEY

From time to time, a solicitor may hold money as a stakeholder, ie pending the outcome of a certain event. For example, in conveyancing, a seller's solicitor may be required by the buyer to hold the deposit as stakeholder as opposed to as agent for the seller. A stakeholder is the principal for both parties and the solicitor is not entitled to hand the deposit money to either party without the consent of the other. Rule 13, n (i)(a) states that clients' money includes stakeholder money. Stakeholder money must therefore be held in a client bank account unless the parties require the solicitor-stakeholder to place the money in a separate account.

Rule 26 requires the solicitor-stakeholder to pay interest, or a sum in lieu of interest, to the person to whom the stake is ultimately paid. This, in turn, depends on the terms upon which the stake is held. In any event, this is subject to r 27(2), which provides that the solicitor, client and other party may come to a different arrangement regarding interest on stakeholder money by a written agreement. In addition, it should be noted that, n (ii) to r 27 indicates that '*in principle* a solicitor is entitled to make a reasonable charge to the client for acting as a stakeholder in the client's matter' (emphasis added). Note (iii) to r 27 then offers the alternative that the agreement between the parties could provide that solicitors are entitled to the interest on the stake to cover their charges, provided that this is fair and reasonable; a further suggestion is that a maximum for the charge is set with an agreement that any interest earned above this sum be paid to the recipient of the stake. However, the right to charge interest would be precluded if a fixed fee or a fee which cannot be varied upwards has been agreed.

CONTROLLED TRUST ACCOUNTS

Controlled trust accounts are dealt with in detail in Chapter 7. We deal here only with aspects of controlled trust money which relate to interest.

Rule 24(7) states that the r 24 interest provisions do not apply to controlled trust money. This is because the SAR cannot override the general rule of law that a trustee must not benefit from the trust. The solicitor must obtain the best rate of interest and pay the beneficiaries the full amount of interest earned (r 15, n (vi) and r 24, n (x)).

The simplest and safest treatment of controlled trust money is to open a separate designated account for each controlled trust. The SAR allow other options which may ensnare the unwary solicitor.

For example, although under r 15 it is permissible to pay controlled trust money into a general client bank account, solicitors should be aware of the dangers of doing so. Since most banks operate a system of stepped or banded rates of interest, depending on the amounts (whereby higher balances attract higher rates of interest), there is a possibility that the deposit of controlled trust funds may take the balance of the general client bank account into a higher rate band. Should this happen, the firm should account to the beneficiaries for the extra interest earned on *all* funds in that bank account because, without the controlled trust money, the higher rate would not have been earned.

Another possibility under the Rules is to have a separate general client bank account specifically for controlled trust money, but this creates the problem of allocating the interest earned between the individual controlled trusts whose funds have been deposited in such a general client bank account (r 15, n (vi)).

OTHER TRUST MONEY

If a solicitor holds money as a trustee, it will be either controlled trust money or client money (r 13, n (vii)). Therefore, a solicitor who is a trustee of a non-controlled trust, will be bound by the Part C obligations because such money is defined as clients' money. A common situation is for the solicitor to be a trustee with others outside the firm and to hold money by virtue of a retainer as trust solicitor.

A rarer situation is where a solicitor, who is trustee with others outside the firm, holds money not by virtue of a retainer as trust solicitor but by virtue of personal appointment as trustee. In these cases the SAR will not apply (r 4, n (iii)). However, charging a fee for the work as trustee or use of the practice stationery may be indications that the position is not held in a personal but a professional capacity (r 4, n (iii)).

APPEAL TO THE LAW SOCIETY

Any client who believes that a solicitor has not discharged the obligations under Part C may apply to the Society for a certificate as to whether interest, or a payment in lieu of interest, is due (r 28(a)). Rule 28, n (i) states that applications must be made direct to the Office for the Supervision of Solicitors (OSS). The OSS may require the solicitor to obtain an interest calculation from the relevant bank or building society. Once the Society certifies that an amount is due, the solicitor must then pay this sum to the client (r 28(b)).

EXERCISES

1. When must a solicitor account to the client for interest on a designated bank account?

2. When must a solicitor make a payment to a client in lieu of interest in respect of money paid into a general client bank account?

3. What is the appropriate rate of interest in calculating the sum due to the client?

4. What are the tax implications of interest on client money (a) for the solicitor and (b) for the client?

5. A solicitor holds money in a general client bank account on which the bank pays interest of 3% after agreeing with the solicitor that it will not charge the solicitor for operating either the office bank account or the client bank account. If a separate designated bank account had been opened for the client, the bank would have credited interest at a rate of 4%. What, if any, is the sum in lieu of interest if:

    (a)   £23,000 is held for 8 days;

    (b)   £20,000 is held for 13 days;

    (c)   £11,000 is held for 15 days;

    (d)   £12,000 is held for 16 days?

Chapter 9

Ensuring compliance with the SAR

INTRODUCTION

There are various measures which aim to ensure that solicitors comply with the SAR. These range from internal controls and procedures to the external review of the accounting records by independent accountants. We start by looking at the most basic internal check which solicitors are required to perform on a regular basis – reconciling the bank statement with the cash account or cash book.

BANK RECONCILIATIONS

A firm's cash book or cash account should contain entries for all the receipts and payments which pass through its bank account. To check that the firm's cash book entries are complete and accurate requires a detailed comparison of the entries on the bank statement with the entries in the cash book. This detailed comparison is also a check on the accuracy of the bank statement. This comparison is known as a bank reconciliation. Solicitors are required to prepare a reconciliation of client bank accounts at least every five weeks in the case of most client bank accounts. The exception to this is where controlled trust money is held in a passbook-operated designated bank account, in which case the reconciliations are required only every 14 weeks.

The first step in preparing a bank reconciliation statement is to compare the items in the cash account with those on the bank statement. Entries appearing in both cash account and bank statement are ticked off. Unticked items may represent:

■ payments on the bank statement which have been omitted from the cash book, eg direct debits, standing orders, bank charges;

■ receipts on the bank statement which have been omitted from the cash book, eg where clients have paid by bank transfer;

■ errors made in the book-keeping of the business;

■ errors made in the book-keeping of the bank;

■ payments in the cash book which are not on the bank statement because the cheque has not been presented by the payee or has been presented but has yet to clear;

■ receipts in the cash book which are not on the bank statement, eg uncleared deposits.

With the exception of those caused by delays in the banking process or errors by the bank, all discrepancies should require corrections to the book-keeping entries in the ledger accounts, before preparing the bank reconciliation.

EXAMPLE

The following information relates to Bill, Ben & Co for the month of December:

CASH BOOK				
Date	Narrative	DR	CR	Balance
1 Dec	Balance			2,000 DR
4 Dec	Cheque no 11		300	1,700 DR
9 Dec	Cheque no 12		450	1,250 DR
9 Dec	Deposit	700		1,950 DR
15 Dec	Cheque no 13		150	1,800 DR
16 Dec	Deposit	400		2,200 DR
22 Dec	Cheque no 14		890	1,310 DR
23 Dec	Deposit	950		2,260 DR
30 Dec	Cheque no 15		320	1,940 DR
30 Dec	Deposit	300		2,240 DR
31 Dec	Cheque no 16		660	1,580 DR

BANK STATEMENT				
		Payments	Receipts	Balance
		£	£	£
December				
1	Balance b/d			2,000 CR
6	Cheque no 11	300		1,700 CR
11	Lodgement		700	2,400 CR
	Cheque no 12	450		1,950 CR
17	Cheque no 13	150		1,800 CR
18	Lodgement		400	2,200 CR
24	Cheque no 14	890		1,310 CR
27	Lodgement		950	2,260 CR
	Standing order	120		2,140 CR
28	Direct credit		100	2,240 CR
31	Bank charges	200		2,040 CR

As the two records do not correspond, we need to make the necessary adjustments to the cash book for December. Only then can we go on to prepare the bank reconciliation statement as at the end of December.

> Payments on the bank statement not in the cash book:
>
> Standing order   £120
>
> Bank charges   £200
>
> Receipts on the bank statement not in the cash book:
>
> Direct credit   £100

With this information the cash book can be corrected:

CASH BOOK				
Date	Narrative	DR	CR	Balance
1 Dec	Balance	2,000		2,000 DR
4 Dec	Cheque no 11		300	1,700 DR
9 Dec	Cheque no 12		450	1,250 DR
9 Dec	Deposit	700		1,950 DR
15 Dec	Cheque no 13		150	1,800 DR
16 Dec	Deposit	400		2,200 DR
22 Dec	Cheque no 14		890	1,310 DR
23 Dec	Deposit	950		2,260 DR
30 Dec	Cheque no 15		320	1,940 DR
30 Dec	Deposit	300		2,240 DR
31 Dec	Cheque no 16		660	1,580 DR
27 Dec	Standing order		120	1,460 DR
28 Dec	Direct credit	100		1,560 DR
31 Dec	Bank charges		200	1,360 DR

The remaining differences (the other unticked items) are caused by the time taken for recipients of cheques to present them for payment or for presented cheques to clear the banking system.

> Unpresented cheques (payments in the cash book not on the bank statement):
>
> Cheque no 15   £320
>
> Cheque no 16   £660
>
> Outstanding lodgements (receipts in the cash book not on the bank statement):
>
> lodgement on 30 December £300

A bank reconciliation statement as at 31 December can then be prepared:

	£	£
Balance per bank statement		2,040
Less: outstanding cheques		
Cheque no 15	320	
Cheque no 16	660	(980)
		1,060
Add: outstanding lodgement		300
Balance per cash book		1,360

The balance on the client cash book must also be reconciled with the total balances of the client ledger accounts. It is important that only credit balances on the client ledger accounts are included. If debit balances are included, they will be netted off against the credit balances and the deficiency in the client bank account will be hidden.

Under r 29 the Society has issued Guidelines for Procedures and Systems for Accounting (Appendix 3 to the SAR 1998). These Guidelines do not override the SAR or detract from the need to comply fully with the SAR. However, solicitors cannot simply ignore these Guidelines on the grounds that they do not carry the same authority as the rules themselves since reporting accountants are required to report material departures from the Guidelines.

The Guidelines emphasise the importance of the bank reconciliations. They require solicitors to have systems which have procedures:

- to maintain a central list or register of all client accounts, both general bank accounts and separate designated bank accounts, to ensure that all bank balances are taken into account;

- to operate a system to ensure that accurate reconciliations are carried out with the required regularity;

- to exclude any debit balances on the client ledger accounts from the reconciliations;

- to produce a full list of unpresented cheques;

- to produce a list of outstanding lodgements;

- to present the reconciliations as formal statements;

- to ensure that a partner checks the reconciliation and any corrective action which may have been taken, and that inquiries are made into any unusual or apparently unsatisfactory items or unresolved matters.

The reconciliations are more than a purely administrative matter. The effectiveness of the reconciliation procedure is dependent upon how seriously those responsible for performing the reconciliation and checking its accuracy take their responsibilities. To be completely effective, the reconciliation must take into account the previous reconciliation statement. It is vital to check that any outstanding items appearing on the previous reconciliation are cleared by the next bank reconciliation or that the delay in presenting the items is investigated if this seems unusual.

OTHER PROCEDURES AND SYSTEMS FOR ACCOUNTING

The SAR imply that accounting records should be kept on the double-entry principle. Rule 32(2) requires all dealings with such money to be entered in a client cash account *and* a client ledger account. The Guidelines in Appendix 3 to the SAR are more explicit. Paragraph 2.3 states that the ledger accounts should be maintained on the double-entry principle and kept legibly and up to date. Note (i) to r 32 strongly recommends that accounting records are written up on a daily basis for large practices, weekly for smaller practices, and that they should be written up in chronological order, complete with narrative. The current balance should either be shown or be readily ascertainable (r 32(5)). These principles also apply to entries in the office ledger accounts relating to client or controlled trust matters; the need to keep the office side of the client records upon the double-entry principle is implied by r 32(4) and the need to update these records is stated in Appendix 3, para 2.8.

Since a separate ledger account should be maintained for each client, it is necessary that each ledger account contains the name of the client; it should also have a description of the matter on which the solicitor is working (Appendix 3, para 2.4). The systems and procedures apply to client and controlled trust money held in separate designated bank accounts as well as money held in a general client bank account (para 2.5).

The procedures and controls should cover both receipts and payments.

Receipts

There should be procedures to ensure that:

    client and controlled trust money is identified, recorded promptly and banked promptly and properly;

    such money is kept safe prior to banking;

    money which should not be in the client bank account is identified and transferred without delay from the client bank account to the office bank account;

    mixed receipts are properly dealt with in compliance with rr 19-21.

Payments

The procedures over payments should ensure that:

    all withdrawals from the client bank account(s) are properly authorised;

    persons authorising withdrawals ensure that supporting documentation is produced showing the reason and date of the payment;

    the balances on the client ledger accounts are checked to ensure that no debit balances occur on the client money side;

    if a payment is to be made other than out of cleared funds, an adequate assessment of the risk of the incoming cheque not being honoured is made (see our comments in Chapter 8);

- transfers of fees from the client bank account to the office bank account are made at the appropriate time, normally after rendering a bill, and only ever by cheque or transfer in the name of the firm;

- loans between clients are made only with the written authority of both the borrower and the lender.

General

Firms should have in place procedures to ensure that:

- compliance with the SAR is achieved;

- if a computerised accounting system is introduced, its introduction is properly implemented and maintained;

- credit balances in the office column of client ledger accounts are investigated;

- situations which require the payment of interest (and presumably payments in lieu of interest – see Chapter 8) are identified promptly;

- a master list is kept of all client bank accounts and office bank accounts;

- books and records are retained for the appropriate length of time;

- no blank client bank account cheques are pre-signed, cancelled cheques are retained and all unused cheques are stored securely.

ACCOUNTANTS' REPORT RULES

In general, s 34 of the Solicitors' Act 1974 requires every solicitor who handles the money of a client or a controlled trust to produce an accountant's report annually as set out in Part F of the SAR 1998 (r 35). Note that the scope of the reporting accountant's work does not extend to checking compliance with Part C of the SAR except for interest on separate designated accounts and accounts opened on clients' instructions (rr 42(1)(o) and 44(d)).

Although it has long been good practice for accountants to arrange for the provision of a letter of engagement, it is now a requirement for the solicitor to provide such a letter to the reporting accountant (r 38(1)). The Society has set out standard terms which are to be incorporated in a letter of engagement to be given by the solicitor to the reporting accountant. The required provisions include whistle-blowing powers: the engagement letter releases the reporting accountant from the duty of confidentiality in certain circumstances. Specifically, the letter instructs and encourages the reporting accountant to report directly to the Society:

- upon the discovery of evidence of fraud or theft of clients' money;

- upon the discovery of matters having a significant bearing on the 'fit and proper' status of the solicitor;

- upon the termination of the accountant's appointment following the issue of, or indication of intent to issue, a qualified report, or the raising of concerns prior to the preparation of the report.

The reporting accountant is also instructed to provide additional information to the Society if requested. The engagement letter must be signed by both accountant and solicitor, each of whom must keep a copy for three years.

The qualifications required of the reporting accountant are competence, independence and integrity. Rule 37 specifies:

(a) Competence: reporting accountants must be members of one of the Institutes of Chartered Accountants (in England and Wales, Scotland or Ireland), the Association of Chartered Certified Accountants or the Association of Authorised Public Accountants and must be registered auditors.

(b) Independence: reporting accountants must not be partners or employees of the solicitor and must disclose any relationship with the solicitor which might impair their independence and specifically if the reporting accountant, or any principal, director, member or employee of the practice:

- is related to the solicitor; or

- has maintained on a regular basis the books of account dealing with clients' money; or

- relies substantially on work referred by the solicitor; or

- is a client or former client of the solicitor; or

- any other matters which might affect an accountant's independence.

   In addition, the solicitor must notify the Society immediately of any change in the appointment of reporting accountant. Presumably, this requirement is to enable the Society to have prior warning of potential difficulties in a solicitor's practice. In the corporate sector, frequent or sudden changes of auditors have been associated with undesirable financial reporting or business practices.

   There is no objection to a solicitor employing an outside accountant to write up the books of account and instructing the same accountant to prepare the annual accountant's report, though this must now be stated in the report.

(c) Integrity: r 37(3) excludes those who have been disqualified by the Council of the Law Society from acting as reporting accountants (disqualification is usually on the grounds of misconduct or negligence).

The accountants' report

Accountants' reports must indicate:

- whether all the partners in the firm are covered by the report or whether individual reports are given for each partner;

- the accounting period covered;

- that the accountant has examined the books, accounts and records;

- whether, in so far as an opinion can be based on the limited examination, the accountant is satisfied that the solicitor has complied with Parts A and B, r 24(1) of Part C and Part D of the SAR 1998, except for:

  - breaches (other than trivial breaches) of the SAR which the accountant must specify;

  - matters on which the accountant has not been able to satisfy himself or herself and an explanation of the reason therefor.

- accountants must also specify as at each of the two dates:

  - the liability to clients as shown by the clients' ledger accounts (clients' money columns); and

- the balance of cash held in client bank account(s) after allowance for outstanding cheques and outstanding lodgements (ie the balance of the cash book/account).

The report must be delivered:

■ once during each practice year;

■ within six months of the end of the accounting period to which it relates.

The accounting period to which the report relates:

■ must normally be the last preceding accounting period, but must cover not less than 12 months;

■ should correspond to the period from which the accounts of the solicitor, or firm, are made up.

The accountants' test procedures

The accountant is required (by r 42(1)(f)) to extract, or check extractions of, balances on the clients' money ledger accounts at not fewer than two dates during the accounting period. At each of the selected dates, the accountant must compare the total liabilities to clients shown by the balances on the clients' money ledger accounts with the cash account balance on the client bank account and reconcile that cash account balance with the balances held in the client bank account and elsewhere as confirmed direct to the accountants by the banks or building societies or other financial institutions.

Although reporting accountants may need to inspect files and documents, solicitors may decline to produce certain documents on the grounds of confidentiality. However, in these circumstances the accountants must qualify their report to that effect, setting out the circumstances (r 45).

Unless exceptional circumstances exist, the place of examination of solicitors' books of account and other relevant documents should be their office, not the office of the accountants (r 40).

The reporting accountants should:

■ Request, and solicitors should provide, details of all bank accounts kept or operated in connection with the solicitors' practice, including client and office bank accounts and other accounts which hold client or controlled trust money (r 41).

■ Examine the book-keeping system to confirm that the accounting system complies with the SAR regarding accounting records and is so designed that:
    - an appropriate ledger account exists for each client and each controlled trust, which shows money received, held or paid on behalf of that person or trust; and
    - clients' money ledger accounts show details of all client money;
    - clients' or controlled trust money is distinguished from office money.

■ Make test checks from the clients' money cash book to the clients' money ledger accounts and test the arithmetical accuracy of both these records.

■ Compare a sample of payments and receipts from the bank statements with those in the clients' money cash book/account.

Test check the system of recording fees and disbursements and of making transfers in respect of these from the client bank account.

Make a test examination of documents to confirm that the transactions comply with Parts A and B of the SAR, and with rr 30-32.

Extract client ledger account balances at not fewer than two dates during the year and at each date:

- compare the total liabilities to clients (the aggregate balance on the clients' money ledger accounts) with the clients' money cash book balance;

- reconcile the cash book balance with the bank statement balance as confirmed direct with the bank or building society.

There is an exception where a computerised accounting system is used. In these cases, the accountant need not check all client ledger balances provided the accountant:

- confirms that a satisfactory system of control is in place and the records balance;

- test checks with individual client ledger balances; and

- states in the accountant's report that this exception has been relied upon.

Ensure that the regular reconciliations have been made and kept by the solicitor.

Make a test examination to see whether payments have been made on behalf of an individual client in excess of money held for that client.

Check the office ledger accounts, office cash accounts and office bank statements to see whether any client money or controlled trust money has been improperly paid into an office bank account or, if properly paid in, has been kept in the office bank account in breach of the SAR.

Check that money withheld from the client bank account on the client's instruction has been properly accounted for and that the client has so instructed the solicitor.

Test the clients' money ledger accounts to see whether the appropriate level of detail has been provided by the solicitor when acting for both borrower and institutional lender.

■ For liquidators, trustees in bankruptcy, Court of Protection receivers and trustees of occupational pension schemes, check that the appropriate records have been kept and cross-check the details with client files.

Check that bank statements and passbooks have been kept for joint bank accounts and cross-check the details with client files.

Check that bank statements and passbooks have been kept for clients' own bank accounts operated by the solicitor and cross-check the details with client files.

Check that interest on separate designated client bank accounts and on accounts opened on clients' instructions is appropriately credited.

Seek any information and explanations needed as a result of the checks and tests.

Check that the solicitor has at least the minimum level of professional indemnity insurance cover.

'AUDIT' CHECKLIST

Although the Society requires accountants to exercise professional judgment in devising the 'audit' programme, it has produced a checklist (Appendix 4 to the SAR 1998), which has to be completed and signed by the accountant. The accountant and solicitor are both required to keep the completed checklist for three years and to produce it to the Society on request.

The checklist of accountants' procedures must be completed (ie the accountant must tick a yes/no box and, if 'no', say whether or not the matter should be noted in the accountant's report). The checks are designed to test compliance with the SAR and with the Accounting Guidelines in Appendix 3.

Accountants must also cross-reference the checklist to their working papers. This will enable subsequent checking to see whether sufficient work was done to justify the conclusion reached. In addition, accountants will have to report the details of unsatisfactory results in a separate section of the checklist and will, in these cases, have to consider whether their report needs to be qualified.

Although a solicitor may agree with the accountant that the accountant may send the report to the Law Society, the responsibility for delivery is that of the solicitor (r 47, n (iii)). The responsibility to deliver the accountant's report rests on the individual solicitor, even if the accountant fails to produce the report to the solicitor within six months of the year end. The deadline is applied strictly. Late filing means that the solicitor must give notice of intention to apply for the next practising certificate and must provide a certificate of good standing by two other solicitors and pay a processing fee of £50.

If it seems likely that the report will be late if sent by post, a solicitor should fax it and then submit a confirmation copy by post. If the report is not going to be available on time, it is possible to request in advance an extension of up to one month, provided there is no previous history of late filing.

NON-COMPLIANCE WITH THE RULES

The Law Society relies on reporting accountants and also visits from its Monitoring Unit to monitor compliance with SAR. These visits have disclosed numerous breaches and failures, not only by solicitors but also by reporting accountants. Compliance with the SAR is the responsibility of all the partners in a practice (r 6 and see *M A Weston v Law Society* (1998)).

Common failures

Omitting the word 'client' from the title of the bank account is a frequent breach, especially in the case of designated accounts. This also results in a breach of r 3, since client money has not been paid into a client bank account.

Sometimes solicitors open building society share accounts in breach of the SAR. Although these accounts may pay a higher rate of interest, they rank after ordinary deposit accounts if the building society is wound up. Share and other accounts should only be used if the client gives a specific instruction.

Reconciliations

Failures in reconciliations include:

- failure to reconcile designated deposit accounts;
- debit balances included in reconciliations;
- the same items regularly appear as reconciling items without further inquiry.

A number of accountants' reports are received which are qualified by reference to trivial breaches but which show a significant difference between liabilities to clients and balances in the clients' bank accounts. If the double-entry principle has been applied correctly, there should never be a difference. Where a difference is reported, an explanation must be given by either the solicitor or the reporting accountant (r 47, n (vi)).

Credit balances on office side of client ledger accounts

The appearance of a credit balance on the office column of a client ledger account is usually an indication of a breach of the SAR. Common examples are the payment into the office bank account of money from a client *before* a bill has been submitted or before disbursements have been incurred. Such money is, of course, client money and should have been paid into the client bank account.

Writing off small balances

Small balances on client account are often 'written off', ie transferred from the client bank account to the office bank account. A solicitor should always obtain the Law Society Council's permission before writing off a balance, no matter how small the balance. In respect of clients' money, there is no 'de minimis' rule.

Powers of the Council

The rules regarding compliance are set out in Part E of the SAR 1998 (r 34):

■ the council may require production of any books and records of a solicitor;

■ a solicitor must comply with such a requirement from the Council;

■ an inspection under r 34 overrides any confidence or privilege between solicitor and client (r 34, n (ii)). The Council does not disclose the reason for a visit by the Monitoring Unit (r 34, n (iv)).

EXERCISES

1. The cash book for the general client account in a solicitor's practice is as follows:

		DR	CR	Balance
1 May	Balance brought forward			100 DR
2 May	Cash deposit	10		110 DR
5 May	Cash deposit	20		130 DR
6 May	Cash deposit	130		260 DR
8 May	Cheque 011452		20	240 DR
10 May	Cheque 011453		30	210 DR
25 May	Cheque 011454		40	170 DR

But the bank statement shows:

		Payments	Receipts	Balance
1 May	Balance brought forward			100 CR
4 May	Deposit		10	110 CR
15 May	Cheque 011452	20		90 CR
19 May	Cheque 011453	30		60 CR
25 May	Bank charges	5		55 CR

Provide a statement reconciling the two balances.

2. The cash book for the general client account of a solicitor is as follows:

		DR	CR	Balance
1 Nov	Balance b/f			500 DR
5 Nov	Cheque 026911*		100	400 DR
8 Nov	Deposit	100		500 DR
15 Nov	Cheque 038522		80	420 DR
16 Nov	Cheque 038523		90	330 DR
18 Nov	Deposit	50		380 DR
20 Nov	Deposit	60		440 DR

* This is a cheque drawn on the office bank account wrongly entered by the cashier as drawn on the client bank account.

The bank statement items are:

		Payments	Receipts	Balance
1 Nov	Balance b/f			500 CR
11 Nov	Deposit		100	600 CR
20 Nov	Cheque 038522	80		520 CR
20 Nov	Bank interest on general account		35	555 CR

Show the bank reconciliation statement.

3. Babb & Co is a client for whom you act in a variety of matters. You agree to deal with the planned redundancy of 50 staff at their Somerset depot. After several months, all matters are resolved and you send Babb & Co a bill on 1 March for £5,000 + VAT.

Babb & Co dispute the bill, pointing out that since five members of the depot left voluntarily, you only dealt with 45 redundancies and that it therefore is entitled to a 10% reduction of the bill. You agree and send a credit note on 31 March. Babb & Co then send a cheque for £5,287.50 on 6 April.

Show the Babb & Co ledger account to reflect the above transactions.

4. Your firm acts under a power of attorney for an aged client, Mrs Beckenridge, for whom no money is currently held. Your terms of business state that money held may be used to reimburse the office account for disbursements made on behalf of the client. During February, you deal with the following matters:

February

  1 Pay £100 for Mrs Beckenridge's electricity account.

  2 Pay £58 bill from her local grocers.

  3 Pay £300 for her nursing home fees.

  8 Receive £550 from Mrs Beckenridge from which money you reimburse the office for previous disbursements.

  28 Send Mrs Beckenridge a bill for your fees for £50 plus VAT and account (ie pay the balance) to her for the money due after paying your bill.

Show how these matters would be recorded in Mrs Beckenridge's ledger account.

5. Your firm acts for the Midshires Building Society, who have agreed to make an advance of £50,000 to Mr and Mrs Yard. They are represented by another solicitor and have agreed that your fees for acting for the lender may be deducted from the mortgage advance.

You receive the mortgage advance on 15 March. On 18 March you raise a bill for £200 plus VAT and pay the mortgage advance (less your fees) to the borrowers' solicitors.

Write up the account of the Midshires Building Society.

6. Your firm acts for a firm of accountants, Maloney & Co, who have difficulty in collecting some of their debts. Record the following transactions in the ledger account of Maloney:

January

  3 Maloney send you a cheque for £100 on account of fees and disbursements.

  4 Proceedings are issued in the County Court against Davis & Co for an unpaid bill. A court fee of £100 is paid.

  5 Similar proceedings are issued against Evans & Co for an unpaid bill. A court fee of £100 is paid.

  6 Francis, one of Maloney's debtors, pays you £250 in cash following an earlier letter by your firm concerning an unpaid fee owed to Maloney & Co. At Maloney's urgent request this is paid to them the same day.

  15 Evans & Co pay you £5,950, which Maloney agrees to accept in full and final settlement.

  22 Davis & Co pay you a cheque of £230 and, as this is made payable to Maloney & Co it is handed over to them.

  31 You send Maloney a bill for the work done in January of £400 plus VAT and disbursement being the second court fee of £100. After making the transfer to the office from the client bank account, you pay the balance held to Maloney & Co.

7. You are instructed by Mr and Mrs Wilson in their sale of a property valued at £69,950 and the purchase of another property costing £81,500. Their existing mortgage with the Loyal Bank is to be redeemed and a new loan of £34,500, also from the Loyal, has been arranged. You also act for the Loyal.

The details of the transactions are as follows:

2 September   Received £100 from Mr and Mrs Wilson on account of fees and disbursements.

2 September   Paid fee for office copies of £10.

6 September   Paid City Council search fee £55.

22 September   Received deposit on sale £6,995.

22 September	Paid deposit on purchase £6,995, the seller having agreed to accept less than 10% of the purchase price.
22 September	Paid Land Registry search fee £4.
22 September	Paid bankruptcy search fee £2.
23 September	Sent final bill of £600 plus VAT to clients with a statement showing the balance required from them to enable the completion of the sale and purchase.
26 September	Received balance due from clients to complete sale and purchase.
26 September	Received mortgage advance from the Loyal Bank of £34,500.
30 September	Paid bill by deduction.
30 September	Received balance of sale price of £62,955.
30 September	Paid balance of purchase price of £74,505.
30 September	Paid estate agent's invoice addressed to Mr and Mrs Wilson of £699.50 plus VAT £122.41.
30 September	Paid Loyal Bank redemption of £22,825.50.
20 October	Paid stamp duty £815.
27 October	Paid Land Registry fees £150.

Prepare the following:

(a) completion statement showing the balance due from the client to you;

(b) the ledger account to record all the transactions in this matter.

8. You are instructed by Mr and Mrs A F Weldt, the two executors of Mrs Johnson, following the death of the testatrix on 18 March. Under her will she left her estate equally to Mr and Mrs Weldt and their two sons, Michael and John. Mrs Johnson was a resident in a home for the elderly. Her assets and liabilities were as follows:

Assets	£
National Savings Income Bonds	5,000.00
plus arrears of interest to 18 March	81.91
Premium Bonds	10,000.00
Minster Bank current	
(non-interest bearing) account	2,523.48

Liabilities	
Executors' expenses	33.46
Undertaker's bill	1,382.48
Monumental mason's bill	185.88

The transactions in relation to this client's matter are as follows:

28 April	Probate granted.
29 April	Paid undertaker's bill.

3 June	Paid commissioner's fees of £7.
9 June	Paid fees for grant of probate £40.
20 June	Received repayment of income bonds, arrears of interest plus final interest of £13.36 (from 18 March to 19 June).
24 June	Received repayment of premium bonds.
29 June	Paid monumental mason's bill.
29 June	Raised interim bill of £400 fees plus VAT and disbursements and settled this from money recovered to date.
6 July	Received balance of account from the Minster Bank.
12 July	Paid Trustee Act advertisement fees for London Gazette and Evening Echo of £75.20 and £124.55 respectively.
13 Sept	Reimbursed executors' expenses of £33.46.

On 30 September, after approval of estate accounts by executors, you finalise matters as follows: you render a final bill of £100 plus VAT and pay this by deduction; you pay each beneficiary his/her share of the residue plus a payment in lieu of interest on the money which has been held in the firm's general client bank account.

Prepare the following:

(a) The ledger account for the matter prior to calculation of payment in lieu of interest.

(b) Calculation of interest due to the beneficiaries on client moneys using a rate of 3%.

(c) Estate account to show amount due to each beneficiary.

(d) The ledger account for the matter after calculation of payment in lieu of interest and distribution to beneficiaries.

9. Prepare a ledger account for a client matter involving the following transactions:

13 Aug	Your firm is instructed to act for Ms Chang, who has sustained facial injuries when falling through a glass door at her parents' house after tripping on a mat. Ms Chang says she has claimed legal expenses on her household insurance. No fee is taken while you make inquiries with the insurance company. Initial advice is given under the Legal Services Commission's Scheme Claim 10 (formerly Green Form).
12 Oct	Instructed engineer to prepare report on glass door.
23 Nov	Received engineer's report with bill of £117.50 (inclusive of VAT).
11 Dec	Received £117.50 from client and notification that her household insurance would not cover legal expenses in this matter.
12 Dec	Applied for legal aid.
11 Jan	Paid engineer's account.
13 Jan	Legal aid certificate received.
1 Feb	Instructed doctor to prepare medical report.
2 March	Received doctor's report and bill for £90.
4 March	Requested Legal Services Commission to meet Claim 10 costs of £91 plus £15.93 VAT and doctor's fee.
29 March	Received £196.93 from Legal Services Commission, raised internal bill for £106.93 and paid doctor £90.

April-August	Various negotiations (which proved abortive) with Ms Chang's parents' solicitors aimed at negotiating a settlement.
2 Sept	Instructed counsel to advise on evidence and settle pleadings.
14 Oct	Counsel advised to issue.
20 Oct	Application to Legal Services Commission to extend legal aid and for payment, in advance, of disbursement of £150 to cover court fee.
15 Nov	Received £150 from Legal Services Commission.
20 Dec	Issued proceedings and paid court fee of £150.
22 Dec	Received invoice from counsel for £150 (inclusive of VAT).
4 Jan	Instructed photographer to take photographs of the scar.
21 Feb	Received photographer's invoice of £126.31 (inclusive of VAT).
21 Feb	Applied to Legal Services Commission for disbursement funding of photographer's bill.
15 March	Received £126.31 from Legal Services Commission.
23 March	Paid photographer's account.
28 Dec	Sent interim claim for fees of £446 plus £78.05 VAT to Legal Services Commission.
31 Jan	Received £524.05 from Legal Services Commission and raised bill for this amount.
5 Aug	Received settlement offer of £15,000.
29 Aug	Received counsel's advice to accept offer and counsel's fee of £75 (inclusive of VAT).
26 Sept	Wrote to the other side accepting offer of £15,000.00 and setting out fees in the sum of £2,500.00 plus VAT of £437.50 and your various disbursements.
5 Oct	Received from the other side settlement money, fees and disbursements (including counsel's fees).
7 Oct	Reported settlement to Legal Services Commission.
29 Oct	Paid £15,000.00 to the client plus £117.50 for the reimbursement of money received on account; paid counsel £225.00; raised bill for balance of fees due and paid this from money in hand. Notified Legal Services Commission of the conclusion of the matter.

10. Redknapp & Co, solicitors, acted for Scales in the purchase and sale of houses and for the building society from whom a mortgage was obtained. The following events took place:

3 April	Received from Scales £200 on account of fees.
5 April	Paid local search fees of £55 in respect of purchase of 'The Haven' by Scales and bankruptcy search fee of £1.
16 April	The Make Money Building Society intimates that it is prepared to grant a loan of £100,000 on security of 'The Haven' and instructs the firm to proceed.
18 April	Received from Scales £1,500 to enable the deposit to be paid to the seller.

20 April	Exchanged contracts for the sale of Scales' house, 'The Paddock', on which there is an existing mortgage of £20,000, received the deposit (£5,000) as agent, being 10% of the selling price and paid deposit of £6,500 to the seller's solicitors (the seller having agreed to accept a 5% deposit).
27 April	Sent completion statement to buyer's solicitor in respect of 'The Paddock', showing a balance due in respect of the purchase of £45,000.
30 April	Received cheque for £100,000 from the building society.
1 May	Sent financial statement to Scales, showing the balance of money which will be due from him on completion of the sale and purchase, together with a bill of costs (including local search fee £55, bankruptcy search fee £1, stamp duty £1,300, Land Registry registration fee £200, your fees £800 and VAT £140).
6 May	Received from Scales the balance due.
8 May	Completed purchase and sale of properties. The amount due is paid to the building society on the same day.
15 May	Paid stamp duty.
22 May	Paid Land Registry registration fee.
22 May	Made the necessary transfers from the client bank account to the office bank account.

Prepare the client ledger account of Scales, showing all entries necessary to deal with the above events, and prepare a completion statement, suitable for presentation to Scales on 1 May 1999 (showing how the balance of money due on completion is calculated).

11. You are required to record the following entries in the books of Mario & Simone, a firm of VAT-registered solicitors.

2 Jan	Mr Stafford calls in and instructs Mario & Simone to act in the purchase of a freehold property for £100,000. He gives Mario & Simone £250 in cash on account of fees and disbursements.
2 Jan	That same day, Mario & Simone pay a local search fee of £55 and a mining search for a fee of £20 by cheques drawn on the client bank account.
10 Jan	Mr Stafford pays Mario & Simone £15,000 towards the purchase price.
22 March	Contracts are exchanged and Mario & Simone send the seller's solicitor a cheque for the deposit of £10,000.
26 March	Mario & Simone send Mr Stafford their bill for fees and disbursements and a completion statement including fees plus VAT.
31 March	Mario & Simone obtain from Mr Stafford a cheque for £1,310, the balance shown on the completion statement.
31 March	The Easylend Building Society send Mario & Simone the mortgage advance cheque of £85,000 which is net of the Society's solicitors' fees, (the Society is represented by another firm).
14 April	Mario & Simone complete the purchase, paying by cheque, £90,000, to the seller's solicitors being the balance of the purchase price.

24 April	Mario & Simone pay stamp duty of £1,000.
29 April	Mario & Simone pay a Land Registry fee of £150.
29 April	Mario & Simone appropriate to themselves their fees and other moneys which are due to them.

In addition you are required to calculate the payment in lieu of interest due to Mr Stafford at the conclusion of the matter. Use a rate of 5% pa.

12. The accountants' checklist can be usefully employed to test familiarity with the SAR 1998 and related Appendices. Against each check, students should enter the reference to the appropriate rule or Guideline which requires solicitors to keep the relevant record or to perform a particular control and the rule which requires accountants to check solicitors' compliance. (Note that only those checks which relate to client money and controlled trust money are included; other checks on, for example, joint accounts or clients' own accounts, are not included.) For example, the first check is for compliance with the principle in r 1(g) and r 32 and the check is required by r 42(1)(a)(iii).

Accountants' check	Check of solicitors' compliance with:	Check required by:
Do the records satisfactorily distinguish between client and controlled trust money and other moneys dealt with by the firm?	r 1(g) and r 32	r 42(1)(a)(iii)
Is a separate ledger account maintained for each client and controlled trust including those where money is held in a separate designated account?		
Do the client ledger accounts show the current balance at all times or is it easily ascertainable?		
Is a record (either a central record or a file of copies) of all bills of costs maintained?		
Are postings from cash book to ledger accounts correct?		
Are casts of cash book and ledger accounts correct?		
Have postings been correctly dated in chronological order?		
Do samples of items on the bank statements correspond to the cash book?		
Do details from paid cheques correspond to entries in the cash book?		

Accountants' check	Check of solicitors' compliance with:	Check required by:
Has the accounting system been ascertained and is it suitable?		
Have costs been withdrawn from the client bank account only after a written notification has been sent?		
Has a sample of client files been examined?		
Were all client files requested for examination made available? (If not are details given in the accountant's report?)		
Were all transactions on client files valid and properly authorised?		
Were all transactions on client files correctly recorded in accordance with Part D of the SAR?		
Has the extraction of client ledger balances been checked at no fewer than two dates through the accounting period?		
Has the total of client ledger balances been agreed to the balance on the cash account at each of the two dates?		
Has the balance on the cash account been reconciled with the balance of the client bank account(s) as confirmed directly with the bank and/or building society?		
Have reconciliations been carried out at least every five weeks, or 14 weeks for controlled trust money in a separate designated, passbook-operated bank account?		
Is each reconciliation in the form of a logical statement likely to reveal any discrepancies?		
Have reconciliation statements been retained?		
From a sample of reconciliation statements, do the reconciliations: – include all client bank accounts; – include all client ledger balances; – include no debit balances; include accurate cash account balances; – include accurate client bank account balances being calculated after allowing for all outstanding deposits and payments?		

Accountants' check	Check of solicitors' compliance with:	Check required by:
Is each reconciliation complete without adjusting or balancing entries?		
Has the firm investigated promptly and corrected debit balances on clients' money columns of client ledger accounts?		
Have differences on reconciliations been investigated and corrected promptly?		
Has a sample of payments from the client bank account been tested to ensure that there are no excess withdrawals?		
Has there been a check on the office ledger and cash accounts and bank statements to ascertain whether clients' money has been paid into the office bank account?		
Have credit balances on the office ledger accounts been investigated to ensure that clients' money is not held in the office bank account?		
Have sums not held in the client bank account been identified?		
Has the reason for withholding sums from the client bank account been established?		
Has the client's permission been evidenced in writing?		
Has a sample of client-to-client transfers been examined to ensure compliance with the SAR?		
Has a sample of client ledger accounts been examined in situations where the firm acts for borrower and (institutional) lender in a conveyancing transaction?		

Chapter 10

Book-keeping systems

INTRODUCTION

The principles of book-keeping have already been introduced. The aim of this chapter is to demonstrate how the books of a business or professional practice are used to provide the basis for the financial statements (namely the profit and loss account and balance sheet) which contain important information for the owners and others.

EXAMPLE

The application of book-keeping for businesses can best be explained using an example:

1. a trader starts a business by investing £1,000 into a business bank account;
2. the trader purchases goods for £200;
3. the goods are then sold for £400.

The book-keeper would record these transactions as follows:

1. the first transaction is the initial investment by the owner which is known as the owner's 'capital', this is what the owner can claim from the business were it to be wound up, though of course the claims of creditors must always be settled first;
2. the second transaction involves *cash* exchanged for *goods*;
3. the third transaction involves *goods* exchanged in return for *cash*.

To record these three transactions, four accounts are needed, one for capital, one for cash, one to record the cost of the items purchased and one account to record the value of the items sold:

First transaction

CASH ACCOUNT			
	DR	CR	Balance
Capital: initial investment	1,000		1,000 DR

CAPITAL ACCOUNT			
	DR	CR	Balance
Cash: capital paid in		1,000	1,000 CR

This shows the initial investment in the business. The business, as an entity separate from the person of the trader, owns £1,000 but 'owes' the proprietor (the trader) £1,000.

Second transaction

CASH ACCOUNT			
	DR	CR	Balance
Capital: initial investment	1,000		1,000 DR
Purchases: goods bought		200	800 DR

PURCHASES ACCOUNT			
	DR	CR	Balance
Cash: payment for goods	200		200 DR

This shows the purchase of goods. While the cash balance of the business has decreased by £200, the business has acquired an asset of an equivalent value. Capital remains unchanged, but the owner's investment is now represented by £800 cash and £200 of goods. The capital account remains as:

CAPITAL ACCOUNT			
	DR	CR	Balance
Cash: capital paid in		1,000	1,000 CR

Third transaction

CASH ACCOUNT			
	DR	CR	Balance
Capital: initial investment	1,000		1,000 DR
Purchases: goods bought		200	800 DR
Sales: goods sold	400		1,200 DR

PURCHASES ACCOUNT			
	DR	CR	Balance
Cash: payment for goods	200		200 DR

SALES ACCOUNT			
	DR	CR	Balance
Cash: received for goods sold		400	400 CR

CAPITAL ACCOUNT			
	DR	CR	Balance
Cash: capital paid in		1,000	1,000 CR

This represents the third transaction, the sale of the goods. The business no longer has the asset in the form of goods but instead has additional cash of £400.

At the end of the accounting period, the accounts are 'closed' by transferring the final balances to a trial balance.

TRIAL BALANCE		
	DR	CR
Sales		400
Purchases	200	
Cash	1,200	
Capital		1,000
Total	1,400	1,400

If the totals of the two columns are not the same, this is a sign that an error has been made in the book-keeping, either:

- a debit entry has been made with no corresponding credit entry or vice versa; or
- an arithmetical error has been made in calculating the closing balance on an account; or
- an error has been made in calculating the totals of the trial balance.

The cause of the difference would need to be investigated before we could proceed to drawing up the profit and loss account and balance sheet.

Even if the totals of the two columns are the same, can we assume that the entries in the ledger accounts are correct? The answer is that we must be careful in making this assumption since we need to bear in mind the possibility that the trial balance will not disclose all errors. For example, if no entries are made for a transaction, the debit column and the credit column of the trial balance will be deficient by the same amount, but the totals of the balances in the trial balance will nevertheless agree. Similarly, the columns in the trial balance may agree, even though the entries in respect of a transaction have been recorded in the wrong accounts – for example, if the payment for purchases is credited to the capital account, not the cash account, the balances on both capital and cash accounts will be incorrect. Another possibility (though rare in practice) is that there are two or more errors which exactly cancel each other out.

The way to guard against such errors occurring is to ensure that the accounting system employs adequate checks and balances so that the errors do not occur in the first place (but if they do occur they are detected, investigated and corrected).

Assuming that we have reason to believe that there are no errors in the accounting balances, we can produce two principal, or 'summary', accounting statements, the profit and loss account and balance sheet (these will be covered in the next chapter).

CREDIT TRANSACTIONS

In the modern commercial world many transactions are on credit – for example, legal practices and other professional firms perform services first and are paid later.

EXAMPLE

Bill & Ben are solicitors who have acted for Weed Ltd in a matter. They have completed the work and now deliver a bill for their costs of £2,000 on terms which give the client 28 days to pay. The accounting treatment should reflect the creation of the debt owed to the firm when the bill or fee note is raised.

CLIENT LEDGER ACCOUNT							
Client: Weed Ltd							
Re: Corporate matter							
		Office ledger			Clients' money ledger		
Date	Detail	DR	CR	Balance	DR	CR	Balance
9.11.01	Fees: work billed	2,000		2,000 DR			

FEES ACCOUNT			
Date		DR	CR	Balance
9.11.01	Weed Ltd: bill delivered		2,000	2,000 CR

Notes

1. The debit balance on the client ledger account indicates that the client owes the practice £2,000 – the client is a debtor of the practice.
2. The fees account records the value of all work done and billed which is the source of income for the practice.

When the client pays, the entries will be:

CASH ACCOUNT			
Date	DR	CR	Balance
23.11.01 Weed Ltd: payment of fees	2,000		2,000 DR

CLIENT LEDGER ACCOUNT							
Client: Weed Ltd							
Re: Corporate matter							
		Office ledger			*Clients' money ledger*		
Date	Detail	DR	CR	Balance	DR	CR	Balance
9.11.01	Fees Account: work billed	2,000		2,000 DR			
23.11.01	Cash: fee paid		2,0000	0			

Notes

1. The credit entry in the client ledger account shows that the debt owed by the client has now been settled – the balance is nil.
2. No entry is made in the fees account when the bill is paid. The balance on the fees account will increase as more bills are delivered. At the end of the accounting period, the balance is transferred to the firm's profit and loss account.

The same principle of book-keeping applies to record liabilities as they are incurred in a business. For example, a solicitor accepts an invoice of £50 from a supplier for the delivery of stationery on terms which require settlement in 30 days. A debt is due to the supplier and the accounting records should reflect this, even though initially no cash changes hands.

STATIONERY ACCOUNT			
Date	DR	CR	Balance
Supplier's: goods on credit	50		50 DR

SUPPLIER'S ACCOUNT			
Date	DR	CR	Balance
Stationery: goods supplied on credit		50	50 CR

Notes

1. The debit balance on the stationery account reflects the cost of stationery delivered. As the year progresses, further purchases will be made which will increase this balance. At the end of the year, the balance on this account will be transferred to the profit and loss account, where it will be treated as an expense of the year (see Chapter 11).
2. Each supplier of goods and services on credit requires an individual ledger account. The credit balance on the account reflects the liability of the practice to the supplier, the supplier is a creditor of the firm.

If the solicitor has no money in the bank, an overdraft facility will need to be arranged to enable the supplier's invoice to be paid. There is no entry for the agreement of the overdraft facility but when the invoice is paid the entries are:

CASH ACCOUNT			
Date	DR	CR	Balance
Supplier's: payment to supplier		50	50 CR

SUPPLIER'S ACCOUNT			
Date	DR	CR	Balance
Stationery: goods supplied on credit		50	50 CR
Cash: invoice paid	50		0

Notes

1. The credit balance in the ledger account for cash indicates the liability of the practice to the bank. The bank account is overdrawn – the bank is a creditor of the practice.
2. The payment of the invoice eliminates the debt due to the supplier.

The accounting treatment of credit transactions often causes confusion because it seems strange to treat revenues and expenses as such before there is any movement of cash. However, this is accepted accounting practice. According to the accruals or matching concept, the cost of goods and services consumed in an accounting period should be matched against the revenue earned in that period. Under this concept, it does not matter whether the goods or services have actually been paid for, nor whether the revenue has actually been received in cash. Of course, by introducing amounts as income which have not been received, there is a risk that clients may not pay their debts and appropriate adjustments will need to be made (see the section on bad debts in Chapter 12).

SYSTEMS IN PRACTICE

Although what we have described above is absolutely correct, it is unlikely in practice for it to be possible to enter individually every single transaction in the main ledger accounts. For this reason, most businesses keep subsidiary records to record all the details and then 'post' the totals to the relevant ledger accounts.

These subsidiary records are:

- the day book;
- the cash book;
- the journal.

These are known as books of 'prime entry'.

Day books

To illustrate the use of a day book, let us look at how a solicitor might keep a record of bills delivered. In a simple situation recording the bills delivered to the following clients could be done on an individual basis:

EXAMPLE

FEES ACCOUNT				
Date	Detail	DR	CR	Balance
6.1.02	I Rees		500	500 CR
7.1.02	J Davies		350	850 CR
8.1.02	P Griffiths		850	1,700 CR

CLIENT LEDGER ACCOUNT

Client: I Rees

Re:

		Office Ledger			Clients' Money Ledger		
Date	Detail	DR	CR	Balance	DR	CR	Balance
6.1.02	Fees				500		500 DR

CLIENT LEDGER ACCOUNT

Client: J Davies

Re:

		Office Ledger			Clients' Money Ledger		
Date	Detail	DR	CR	Balance	DR	CR	Balance
7.1.02	Fees				350		350 DR

CLIENT LEDGER ACCOUNT

Client: P Griffiths

Re:

		Office Ledger			Clients' Money Ledger		
Date	Detail	DR	CR	Balance	DR	CR	Balance
8.1.02	Fees				850		850 DR

Thus, all bills delivered would have to be entered individually in the fees account. In practice, where there are many clients and numerous bills being delivered, it would not be convenient to have so many individual entries in the main ledger accounts. A more practical method is to maintain a separate listing of bills delivered (a bills delivered book), the total of which is periodically posted to the fees account.

This list or bills delivered book is contained in a separate print-out (or in a bound book) and is sometimes referred to as a 'day book'. The list is purely a memorandum record and is not a ledger account. Although only the total of the day book is entered in the fees account, we still need to record each bill in the relevant client's account.

Bills delivered book	
	£
I Rees	500
J Davies	350
P Griffiths	850
	1,700

Thus, in the main ledger the accounts will appear as:

FEES ACCOUNT				
Date	Detail	DR	CR	Balance
8.1.02	Debtors: fees from Bills delivered book		1,700	1,700 CR

I Rees (Client) ACCOUNT				
Date	Detail	DR	CR	Balance
6.1.02	Fees	500		500 DR

J Davies (Client) ACCOUNT				
Date	Detail	DR	CR	Balance
7.1.02	Fees	350		350 DR

P Griffiths (Client) ACCOUNT				
Date	Detail	DR	CR	Balance
8.1.02	Fees	850		850 DR

To prevent the main ledger becoming cluttered with many debtor accounts, a summary or total account showing the aggregate clients' balances can be kept in the main ledger (see 'Control accounts', below) with individual clients' accounts kept in a subsidiary ledger.

The cash book

In previous examples we have entered each payment and receipt of cash in the cash account. In practice, it would not be practicable to record hundreds, thousands or even hundreds of thousands of payments and receipts in the main ledger account. So a separate record is kept of all the details – the cash book. This is the first record of all receipts and payments. Typically, it is analysed, ie divided into columns, one for each main item of expense or revenue.

EXAMPLE

The following is an extract from the payments side of the cash book:

CASH PAYMENTS BOOK (extract)							Postings to subsidiary creditors ledger accounts
Date	Payee	Cheque No	Total	Drawings	Creditors		
	ASB Ltd	00114	400		400	→	Debit individual creditor account
	KLM	00115	1,000		1,000	→	Debit individual creditor account
	RAC	00116	100	100			
	SJL & Co	00117	550		550	→	Debit individual creditor account
	Total		2,050	100	1,950		

Postings to main ledger → Credit Cash Account | Debit Drawings Account | Debit Creditors Control Account

The main ledger account for bank and cash is simply a summary of the entries in the cash book itself. It is often posted on a weekly or monthly basis with totals for receipts and payments. The balance on this account represents the money the business has in the bank or owes to the bank.

Many small businesses keep only a cash book. At the end of the year the accountant can make any adjustments required to produce a final set of accounts on an accruals basis.

The journal

The journal keeps a memorandum record of all transactions which are not dealt with in the other books of prime entry.

The typical uses of the journal are:

■ adjustments, eg closing stock and bad debts;
■ correction of errors.

CONTROL ACCOUNTS

A control account summarises the balances on numerous individual accounts, for example, suppliers' or customers' ledger accounts or clients' ledger accounts. The element of control is introduced if one individual is responsible for writing up the control account and another is charged with writing up all the individual accounts. The balance on the control account should equal the total of the balances on the individual accounts; if the two records do not balance, then the difference needs to be investigated. Such comparisons should be performed at regular intervals.

The periodic total of the bills delivered book (or sales day book) is posted to the debit of the clients' (or sales) ledger control account. The periodic total of the cash receipts from clients (debtors) is posted from the analysis column of the cash book to the credit of the clients' (or sales) ledger control account. In addition, a separate subsidiary (or memorandum) set of ledger accounts will contain the individual ledger accounts for each client (or debtor), in which will be recorded the individual bills delivered (or sales) and the cash received from each individual client (or debtor). Of course, if all the entries in both the main ledger accounts and the subsidiary ledger accounts have been made correctly, the balance on the control account should equal the total of all the individual balances on the client ledger accounts.

EXAMPLE

The following extract from the bills delivered book lists the invoices sent to clients:

BILLS DELIVERED BOOK				Postings to subsidiary ledger accounts
Date	Bill Delivered to:	Amount		
	Will	100	→	Debit individual client ledger account
	Dill	200	→	Debit individual client ledger account
	Phil	150	→	Debit individual client ledger account
	Lil	150	→	Debit individual client ledger account
	Total	600		

Posting to main ledger | Credit: fees account
Debit: Client ledger control account

Subsequently, Will pays £80 and Dill pays £150, these sums being recorded in the appropriate column of the cash receipts book.

CASH RECEIVED BOOK (extract)						
Date	Detail	Total	Cash	Sundry	Clients	
	Will	80			80	→ Credit individual client ledger account
	Dill	150			150	→ Credit individual client ledger account
	Total	230			230	

Postings to subsidiary ledger accounts

Postings to main ledger | Debit Cash Account | | | Credit Client Ledger Control Account

The main ledger accounts and subsidiary ledger accounts will appear as follows:

Main ledger accounts

FEES ACCOUNT				
Date	Detail	DR	CR	Balance
	Client ledger control account: Total from Bills Delivered book		600	600 CR

CASH ACCOUNT				
Date	Detail	DR	CR	Balance
	Client ledger control account: Total from Cash Received book	230		230 DR

CLIENT LEDGER CONTROL ACCOUNT				
Date	Detail	DR	CR	Balance
	Fees: Total of Bills Delivered book	600		600 DR
	Cash: Total from Cash Received book		230	370 DR

Subsidiary client ledger accounts

WILL (CLIENT LEDGER) ACCOUNT (subsidiary account)				
Date	Detail	DR	CR	Balance
	Fees	100		100 DR
	Cash		80	20 DR

DILL (CLIENT LEDGER) ACCOUNT (subsidiary account)				
Date	Detail	DR	CR	Balance
	Fees	200		200 DR
	Cash		150	50 DR

PHIL (CLIENT LEDGER) ACCOUNT (subsidiary account)				
Date	Detail	DR	CR	Balance
	Fees	150		150 DR

LIL (CLIENT LEDGER) ACCOUNT (subsidiary account)				
Date	Detail	DR	CR	Balance
	Fees	150		150 DR

To test the arithmetical accuracy of the book-keeping, the control account balance (£370) is periodically compared with the total balances on the individual client accounts. The list of balances is:

Will	20
Dill	50
Phil	150
Lil	150
Total	370

The fact that the control account balance agrees with the total of the individual ledger balances is prima facie evidence of arithmetical accuracy. It will not, however, reveal posting errors – for example, a bill being posted to the wrong client ledger account.

Control accounts can be used to summarise the detailed subsidiary ledger accounts, not only for clients but also for the suppliers or creditors.

EXERCISES

1. Anne commences trading and carries out the following transactions:

    (a) Record all these transactions in the books of Anne.

    (i)   Anne starts with £500 in the bank (being capital paid in).

    (ii)   Anne buys goods for cash costing £500.

    (iii)   Anne sells the goods for £600 cash.

    (iv)   Anne buys goods on credit from Brenda Ltd for £1,000.

    (v)   Anne sells them for £1,200 on credit to Glenda & Co.

    (vi)   Glenda & Co pay £1,200.

    (vii) Anne pays Brenda Ltd £1,000.

    (viii) Anne buys £2,000 of goods from Penny Ltd on credit.

    (ix)   Anne sells them to Thora Ltd for £2,500 on credit.

    (x)   Thora Ltd pays £2,000.

    (xi)   Anne pays Penny Ltd £1,800.

    (b) Draw up a trial balance at the end of the series of transactions.

2. (a)   Make up the accounts of a business to show:

    (i)   Harry, the owner, starts the business off by providing £200 in cash.

    (ii)   Goods are purchased for £50.

    (iii)   Goods are sold for £150 on credit to Biddy.

    (iv)   The following cash payments are made:

    Wages £20

    Rent   £10

    Electricity   £20

    Machinery   £100

    (b) Produce a trial balance after all transactions have been recorded.

3. B Bunter starts off in business by opening a bank account with £500 and agreeing an overdraft limit of £1,000.

    (a) Record this and the following cash transactions in his ledger accounts:

    (i)   Purchase of goods for £500.

    (ii)   Sale of those goods for £1,000.

    (iii)   Payment of wages of £100.

    (iv)   Purchase of a lorry for £1,000.

    (b) Prepare the trial balance.

4. Christopher starts off in business and in the first year makes the transactions listed below.

  (a) Record the following transactions in appropriate ledger accounts:

    (i)   He puts £1,000 of his own money into the business bank account.

    (ii) Amy provides a loan to the business of £2,000 at 10% interest per annum repayable in five years' time.

    (iii) He buys goods for £600 and sells some of them for £700 in cash and the rest for £300 on credit.

    (iv) He pays Amy £200 interest.

    (v)   He purchases a lorry for £2,000.

    (vi) He makes drawings of £500 cash.

  (b) Draw up a trial balance.

5. Explain the function of a trial balance.

6. Describe the types of error which may not be detected by a trial balance.

Chapter 11

From trial balance to final accounts

INTRODUCTION

The last chapter took us as far as the trial balance – the last check on the accuracy of the ledger accounts. The trial balance performs no other function than to test the arithmetical agreement of debit and credit balances. To obtain more information about how the business has fared during the period under review and how it stands at the end of the period we need to rearrange the balances on the ledger accounts into a 'profit and loss account', which provides a calculation of any profit or loss realised during the period, and a 'balance sheet', which shows a picture of the business at a particular point in time.

CLASSIFICATION OF ACCOUNT BALANCES

As we have said, balances on ledger accounts which represent an item of *expense* or *income* which has been incurred or earned during the year are transferred to the profit and loss account, for example, the balance on the wages account represents the cost of labour used; the balance on the heat and light account represents the total paid for energy consumed in the period; the balance on the purchases account represents the total cost of goods purchased for re-sale.

The term 'expenditure' creates the potential for confusion, since expenditure may provide either short-term benefits which have been consumed during the period under review (these are written off against the revenue in the profit and loss account for that period, often called 'revenue expenditure') or long-term benefits (confusingly known as 'capital expenditure'). Capital expenditure relates to items which will provide future economic benefits and these balances appear in the balance sheet. Balances on accounts representing items which will provide future economic benefits are 'assets', for example, a car, a building or machinery. The items representing capital expenditure are also known as 'fixed assets'.

Balances on accounts which represent other assets, such as cash at the bank or debtors will also be transferred to the balance sheet. These items are known as 'current assets' or sometimes by an old-fashioned but none the less descriptive term, 'circulating assets', since these are items which are constantly changing, unlike the fixed assets. Current assets are those items which may be turned into cash or provide some other benefit in the near future (usually the next accounting period).

Balances on accounts representing a future outflow of benefits are known as 'liabilities', for example, creditors, bank overdraft, loans, and unpaid bills. These appear in the balance sheet as a deduction from assets. It is useful to distinguish between short-term and long-term liabilities. The distinction depends on when the debt is payable; short-term liabilities are claims which will have to be settled within 12 months of the balance sheet date. Short-term liabilities are known as 'current liabilities' and are shown as deductions from 'current assets'. Long-term liabilities, such as a bank loan repayable in five years' time, are shown as a final deduction in the balance sheet.

The resulting 'bottom line' or net figure (assets minus liabilities) is known as 'net assets'. The net assets have been financed by the owners' capital, which appears as the final section in the balance sheet. For the balance sheet to balance, the figure for net assets must equal the total of the capital section.

From the trial balance we can proceed to the profit and loss account and balance sheet by categorising the balances. The profit and loss account contains the balances of those accounts which reflect income or expenditure *during* the year. The balance sheet contains the balances of the accounts which reflect the assets, liabilities and capital *at* a particular date; it is often referred to as a 'snap-shot' of the business.

EXAMPLE

Taking the figures from the first example of the last chapter, where the trader started with capital of £1,000, made purchases of goods for £200 and sold the goods for £400, the trial balance was:

	DR	CR
Sales		400
Purchases	200	
Cash	1,200	
Capital		1,000
Total	1,400	1,400

We now have to categorise each of these balances, deciding those which are income, expenses, assets, liabilities or capital. The categorisation will determine the destination of the balance, whether it goes in the profit and loss account or the balance sheet:

	DR	CR	Category	Destination*
Sales		400	Income	P&L
Purchases	200		Expense	P&L
Cash	1,200		Asset	B/S
Capital		1,000	Capital	B/S
Total	1,400	1,400		

* P & L = profit and loss account; B/S = balance sheet.

We can now draw up the final accounts, the profit and loss account and the balance sheet:

Profit and loss account for the period ended on . . .

	£
Sales	400 CR
Less purchases	200 DR
Net profit	200 CR

Balance sheet at . . .

	£
Assets	
Cash	1,200 DR

Financed by:

	£
Capital	1,000 CR
Retained profit	200 CR
	1,200 CR

Note

The final balance on the profit and loss account is added to the capital in the balance sheet, since the profit belongs to the owner of the business. The concept of *profit* refers to the amount which could be consumed by the owner without reducing the capacity of the business. Hence, the trader in the above example could withdraw up to £200 from the business and still leave it at least as well off as it was at the start. The fact that no drawings of profit have been made results in an increase in the size of the business; net assets and capital have grown from £1,000 to £1,200.

OPENING THE BOOKS IN THE SECOND ACCOUNTING PERIOD

Now suppose we start a second accounting period. The ledger accounts will be opened on the first day of the second accounting period with the balances brought forward from the last balance sheet which will be added to or depleted by subsequent transactions in this period. The balances on the ledger accounts which have been transferred to the profit and loss account of the first period will not feature again – they relate to a past accounting period.

EXAMPLE

The ledger accounts at the start of the second period will now appear as:

CASH ACCOUNT			
	DR	CR	Balance
Opening balance			1,200 DR

CAPITAL ACCOUNT			
	DR	CR	Balance
Opening balance			1,000 CR

RETAINED PROFIT ACCOUNT			
	DR	CR	Balance
Opening balance			200 CR

If in this second period the trader purchases goods costing £400 on credit, the entries in the accounts will be:

SUPPLIER ACCOUNT			
	DR	CR	Balance
Purchases		400	400 CR

PURCHASES ACCOUNT			
	DR	CR	Balance
Supplier	400		400 DR

If these goods are then sold for £900 on credit, the entries are:

CUSTOMER ACCOUNT			
	DR	CR	Balance
Sales	900		900 DR

SALES ACCOUNT			
	DR	CR	Balance
Customer		900	900 CR

Suppose finally that the owner takes £400 from the business bank account for personal consumption. The entries to record these drawings are:

CASH ACCOUNT			
	DR	CR	Balance
Opening balance			1,200 DR
Drawings		400	800 DR

DRAWINGS ACCOUNT			
	DR	CR	Balance
Cash	400		400 DR

At the end of this period we close off the accounts and draw up a trial balance:

	DR	CR	Category	Destination
Sales		900	Income	P&L
Purchases	400		Expense	P&L
Supplier		400	Liability	B/S
Customer	900		Asset	B/S
Cash	800		Asset	B/S
Capital		1,000	Capital	B/S
Retained profit		200	Capital	B/S
Drawings	400		Reduction in Capital	B/S
Total	2,500	2,500		

The profit and loss account and the balance sheet can be prepared:

Profit and loss account for the period ended on . . .

	£
Sales	900 CR
Less purchases	400 DR
Net profit	500 CR

Balance sheet at . . .

	£
Assets	
Customer	900 DR
Cash	800 DR
Total assets	1,700 DR

Financed by:	
	£
Capital	1,000 CR
Profit to date	
(ie £200 + £500)	700 CR
Less: Drawings	(400 DR)
Supplier	400 CR
	1,700 CR

The top section of the balance sheet shows the assets of the business, those things expected to provide benefits in the future. We have assumed that the customer will be able to pay per the terms of the sale agreement.

The bottom section of the balance sheet shows how the business has been financed: £1,000 being the original investment of the owner plus the profits of the two periods (less the drawings), plus the provision of goods on credit by the supplier. In practice it is usual to show the liabilities to third parties as a deduction from assets, since these are genuine claims on the assets – the creditors expect to get paid. This presentation gives us:

Balance sheet at . . .	
	£
Assets	
Customer	900 DR
Cash	800 DR
Total assets	1,700 DR
Less:	
Liability to supplier	400 CR
Net assets	1,300 DR
Financed by:	£
Capital	1,000 CR
Profit to date	
(ie £200 + £500)	700 CR
Less: Drawings	(400 DR)
	1,300 CR

CONCLUSION

In this chapter we have shown how the final accounts are prepared from the balances on the ledger accounts. The following general principles may help:

■ Debit balances represent expenses or assets. If debit balances are expenses, they are treated in the profit and loss account. If debit balances are classified as assets (items with some future value or benefit), they are dealt with in the balance sheet.

■ Credit balances represent income, liabilities or capital. Credit balances classified as income or revenue are treated in the profit and loss account. Other credit balances are either capital (finance provided by the owner(s)) or liabilities (finance in the form of cash or of goods and services provided on credit) to third parties and are dealt with in the balance sheet with liabilities usually shown as a deduction from assets.

Or more simply:

DEBIT BALANCES ARE: CREDIT BALANCES ARE:

ASSETS   LIABILITIES

EXPENSES   INCOME

REDUCTIONS IN CAPITAL   CAPITAL
                                       REDUCTIONS IN ASSETS

The format of these final accounts is:

Profit and loss account for the period ended on . . .

Income	CREDITS
Less expenses	DEBITS
= Net profit	CREDIT*

* Unless expenses (debit balances) exceed income (credit balances), in which case a loss has been made.

Balance sheet at . . .

Assets	DEBITS
Less:	
Liabilities	CREDITS
= Net assets	DEBIT
Financed by:	
Capital	CREDIT
Retained profit	CREDIT*
	CREDIT

* Unless losses (debit balances) exceed retained profits (credit balances) in which case the capital is reduced since the owners are the ultimate risk-bearers. If the business is a limited company there may be serious consequences if the capital is reduced and there certainly will be problems should liabilities exceed assets, since the company will be insolvent.

You should bear these principles in mind when attempting the following exercises.

EXERCISES

1. From each of the trial balances prepared in answer to questions 1-4 in Chapter 10, prepare a profit and loss account and balance sheet.

2. Explain why debit balances generally represent either expenses or assets or reductions in capital.

3. Explain why credit balances generally represent either income, liabilities or capital.

4. Explain why profit is added to the owner's capital and why drawings are deducted from capital.

5. Explain what is meant by the term 'net assets' and why net assets must always be equal to the capital section of the balance sheet.

6. Explain what happens to the balances on the ledger accounts at the end of an accounting period and what happens to these same balances at the start of the next accounting period.

Chapter 12

Stock, depreciation and other adjustments

INTRODUCTION

The earlier chapters introduced accounts at a simple level where all transactions involved either cash or credit transactions. In practice, many other types of transactions and events occur which need to be recorded in the accounts. These may best be described as post-trial balance adjustments – adjustments to the final balances after the accounts have been closed. We now explain the more common adjustments. There are of course many other items which will be encountered in the real world, but space prohibits a more extensive coverage in this text. Nevertheless, the following examples illustrate general principles which should be capable of adaptation to different events and conditions.

The main point which each of the following examples demonstrates is the articulation of the profit and loss account with the balance sheet. Each adjustment has one impact on the profit and loss account and one impact on the balance sheet, ie double-entry. The essential lesson to learn is which statement (profit and loss account or balance sheet) is debited and which is credited.

STOCK

A basic accounting system should be able to record the cost of goods purchased by ensuring that all purchase invoices are recorded: debit the purchases account, credit the cash or creditors' accounts. More sophisticated accounting systems are able to record not only the cost of goods purchased but also the cost of goods sold. Major supermarkets use scanners to do this by reading the product bar codes of items sold to customers. This information not only updates the stock records but, in a fully integrated system, also provides an up-to-date record of the cost of the items sold, which is used in calculating the supermarket's profit.

The accounting procedures of the less sophisticated systems are often unable to cope with keeping a running 'book stock' and require a physical stock-take to determine the identity and quantities of the unsold items which remain in stock. Once the stock-take has been completed, the items in stock need to be 'priced' or 'valued', usually by reference to their original purchase cost. The total cost of stock is a figure which needs to be introduced into the accounting records, normally by means of a post-trial balance adjustment made on double-entry principles.

The unsold items clearly represent an asset and so should be included as such in the balance sheet (ie a debit balance is introduced). But where is the credit entry for this adjustment? The answer is: in the profit and loss account. The cost of purchases (a debit balance) must be reduced by the cost of the stock (a credit entry) in order to get a fair matching of revenues and costs and thereby a fair measure of profit.

EXAMPLE

In Chapter 10, Exercise 4, Christopher had made purchases of £600 and sales of £1,000. Now suppose that Christopher had not sold all the purchased items; some which had cost £100 remained unsold at the end of the period (ie the cost of purchases included £100 for items which have not been sold by the period end). Clearly, it would not be right to charge the total cost of purchases against the sales revenue generated by selling only some of those items. An adjustment is required to produce a fair *matching* of costs and revenues. By deducting the cost of closing stock from the purchases figure, we obtain the cost of goods sold (or cost of sales).

Profit and loss account for the period ended . . .

	£	£
Sales		1,000
Less		
Purchases	600	
Deduct cost of unsold goods	(100)	
Cost of goods sold		(500)
Gross profit		500
Less		
Interest		(200)
Net profit		300

	£
Balance sheet at . . .	
Lorry	2,000
Stock	100
Debtors	300
Bank	400
Less	
Loan	(2,000)
Net assets	800
Financed by:	
	£
Capital	1,000
Add: Net profit	300
Less: Drawings	(500)
	800

Note the effect of allowing for the cost of unsold stock is to increase profit *and* the value of net assets. The double-entry is:

> credit the profit and loss account,
>
> debit the balance sheet.

Essentially, costs or expenses incurred in the first period are taken out of the profit and loss account (purchases are reduced) and are carried forward to the next accounting period as an asset in the balance sheet.

Accounting for stock is one of the most difficult areas for students to understand. We think that it is worth emphasising this point through another example.

EXAMPLE

A street trader starts in business with £200 capital and buys 100 silk ties for a total cost of £100. In the first week of trading 80 ties are sold at £1.25 each, a total of £100. What is the profit for the week?

Although it might be tempting to say that there has been no profit or loss (£100 out, £100 in), to deduct the cost of 100 ties from the revenue generated from the sale of 80 ties is not a fair measure of the profit made; the trader makes a profit of 25p on every tie sold. Since the trader still has 20 ties in stock, the cost of these needs to be accounted for (assuming there is a reasonable prospect that these can be sold in the future). The final accounts will need to reflect the adjustment required to account for the stock.

Profit and loss account for the period ended on . . .

	£	£
Sales (80 ties @ £1.25)		100
Less		
Purchases (100 ties @ £1.00)	100	
Deduct: Stock of 20 ties (@ £1.00)	(20)	
Cost of ties sold (80 ties @ £1.00)		(80)
Gross profit (80 ties costing £1.00 each, sold for £1.25 = profit of)		20

Balance sheet at . . .

	£
Stock	20
Cash	200
	220
Financed by:	
	£
Capital	200
Profit	20
	220

Let us take this example into a second accounting period. Assume that the trader is so pleased with the first week's results that a second batch of purchases is made: 200 ties at a total cost of £200 and during the second week of trading all 220 ties are sold for a total of £275. The profit and loss account for the second week and the balance sheet at the end of that week will appear as:

Profit and loss account for the period ended on . . .

	£	£
Sales (220 ties @ £1.25)		275
Less		
Opening stock (20 ties @ £1.00)	20	
Purchases (200 ties @ £1.00)	200	
Cost of ties sold (220 ties @ £1.00)		(220)
Gross profit (220 ties costing £1.00 each, sold for £1.25 = profit of)		55

	Balance sheet at . . .	
		£
Cash		275
		275
		£
Financed by:		
Capital		200
Profit to date		75
		275

If stock had been ignored even though it existed at the end of the first week the profit and loss account would have shown neither a profit nor a loss; £100 was received from the sale of the ties and £100 was paid for the purchases. In the second week the profit and loss account would have shown a profit of £75; £275 was received from the sales of ties and £200 was paid for purchases. Under both approaches the profit is the same in total (£75), but the recognition of the profit in each period is different. Accounting for stock has the effect of delaying recognition of expenses until the related assets are sold (the cost of the unsold purchases is carried forward to be treated as expenses in the next accounting period when the stock is sold).

The effect on profit of accounting for closing stock makes this one of the most common of management frauds; stock is deliberately and fraudulently *over*stated in order to overstate profit – the yardstick for measuring management performance. This type of fraud is often most likely when:

- an element of management remuneration is based on a percentage of profits;
- existing owners/managers are seeking a buyer for the business; or
- real profits are below the expectations of the stock market or a higher level of senior management (eg where a subsidiary reports to a parent company).

One method of inflating the value of closing stock is to price it at selling price rather than the original cost (provided, of course, that it can be sold at a profit, ie selling price is above cost). To prevent such inflation of stock values, the standard valuation principle is to value stock at the lower of cost and 'net realisable value' (defined as selling price less any additional costs). Thus, in the above example the selling price of the silk ties was £1.25 per tie but the stock at the end of the first week was valued at the lower figure of the purchase cost of £1.00 per tie. To have valued the stock at the selling price would have been to anticipate a profit which has not yet been realised, since the stock has not yet been sold.

If, for some reason, the expected selling value was 50p per tie, ie a total of, say £10, then this would be the relevant figure for stock, effectively recognising the expected loss on the future sales (ties which cost £1.00 each could only be sold for 50p). This is an application of the accounting concept of 'prudence' which states that profits should not be anticipated but losses should be recognised when they become foreseeable.

Of course, there may be tax implications for the overstatement of accounting profit which raises an alternative possibility that management may be more inclined to understate profit in order to minimise tax liabilities. Either way, accurate accounting for stock is a prerequisite for accurate financial reporting.

WORK-IN-PROGRESS

In a legal and any other professional firm, the equivalent of a trader's stock is work-in-progress. This is best defined as the cost of incomplete work which has not been billed. In theory, the accounting treatment for work-in-progress is exactly the same as for stock, although there is no concept of gross profit (closing work-in-progress is deducted from office expenses and opening work-in-progress is added to such expenses).

In practice, however, there are significant difficulties in attributing a 'value', particularly in a legal practice, for several reasons. A partly completed file in a professional firm may well be different in kind from, say, partially completed widgets or cans of beans. On top of this, a solicitor's contract with the client is usually an 'entire contract' which cannot be valued until it is completed satisfactorily, compared against the original instructions and judged against the statutory billing criteria. Therefore, it if is not completed at the year end (or possibly before the accounts are drawn up), it can be argued that it has no 'net realisable value'. For this reason, many law firms have placed a 'nil' value on work-in-progress. In an established practice, the omission has no effect on the profit and loss account, provided the firm bills consistently and there is no significant change in the level of work-in-progress, since opening and closing work-in-progress cancel each other out.

However, following the windfall tax provisions of the Finance Act 1998 (ss 42-46 and Sch 6) the accounts of professional firms have to show 'a true and fair view' in calculating their taxable profits for accounting periods beginning after 6 April 1999 (see the guidance issued by the Law Society: *Gazette* 20 January 1999, pp 36-37). The arguments about whether it is now necessary also to show a figure for work-in-progress in calculating profits for tax purposes on a 'true and fair basis' (and if so at what valuation) are complex and a comprehensive treatment of this subject is outside the scope of this text. It is made more complex by two further issues: 'interim billing' and the fact that clients are increasingly requiring law firms to share risk with them with regard to fees – for example, in connection with conditional fee work. On the latter issue, the Inland Revenue have conceded that it may not be necessary to value work-in-progress because the fee outcome is not known until the work is completed. However, this same argument can be applied to all legal work. With regard to interim billing, it is established law that, unless there is a divisible contract, an interim bill does not have to be brought into account in the year it is raised because it is on account of the final (or statute) bill. Nevertheless, most law firms include interim bills as part of their income. These firms should look very carefully at this matter.

DEPRECIATION

The concept of depreciation is familiar to most of us, in the sense that we are aware that the value of most of our possessions will decline as time passes. In an accounting context, depreciation is charged as an expense against profit in order to write off the original *cost* of a fixed asset over its expected useful life.

The charging of depreciation is another example of the application of the matching concept. It would not be fair to treat as an expense the cost of a new asset acquired during one particular accounting period. To do so would overstate the expenses of the year of acquisition and understate the value of assets in the balance sheet at the end of that accounting period. Furthermore, the expenses of future years would be understated because they would not include the relevant portion of the fixed asset even though it was being used to generate profits in those future years. Spreading the cost of the fixed asset (over the years expected to benefit from its use) ensures that a portion of the cost is charged in each of the years expected to benefit.

Depreciation is just as much a charge in the profit and loss account as wages, rent, heating or telephone – except, of course, that it does not represent an outflow of cash in each of the years. The initial cost of the fixed asset involves a cash outflow. Subsequent charging of depreciation involves no cash outflow. Depreciation is therefore referred to as a non-cash expense which involves making a 'book entry'.

The effects of depreciation are:

- To charge part of the original cost as an expense in the profit and loss account. The charge for depreciation will reduce the profit figure, which in turn will reduce the amount of profit available for distribution and will retain funds which might otherwise be distributed (ie maintains the capital of the business).
- To reduce the net book value of the fixed asset in the balance sheet which shows the unexpired portion of the original cost of the asset.

Calculating depreciation

There are several possible methods for estimating the annual charge for depreciation. Two of the more common are the 'straight line' method and the 'reducing balance' method.

The straight line method

This method charges an equal amount to each of the years expected to benefit from its use. The calculation of the annual depreciation charge is: cost of asset less (expected scrap value at end of life) divided by expected life in years, ie:

$$\frac{\text{COST} - \text{SCRAP}}{\text{EXPECTED LIFE}}$$

Having calculating the depreciation charge, we then need to make an adjustment (post-trial balance) to debit the profit and loss account with the charge for the year and to credit a 'provision' account in the balance sheet with the same amount. This provision account accumulates the annual charges against profit as time goes by and is shown in the balance sheet as a deduction from the cost of the asset. The resulting net figure is known as the net book value (ie original cost less depreciation charged to date). As time passes, the provision for accumulated depreciation grows (for example, Provision in Year 1 = Charge in Year 1; Provision in Year 2 = Charge in Year 1 + Charge in Year 2 and so on) until, at the end of the expected life of the asset, the book value has been reduced from its original cost to the initial estimate of its eventual scrap value. An important point to note is that at no time is there any claim that the book value actually reflects the current market or resale value; accounting is based on the historical cost convention, which records the results of past transactions rather than current values. Thus, by charging depreciation, all we are attempting to do is to write off the original cost of the asset over the number of years expected to benefit from its use.

EXAMPLE

Suppose that a motor vehicle was purchased on 1 January 1999 for £20,000, when it was anticipated that it would be used in the business until 31 December 2002, at which date it would be sold for £4,000.

The profit and loss account for each year of the asset's life will be charged with:

$$\frac{(£20,000-£4,000)}{4} = £4,000$$

Profit and loss account extracts – for years ended 31 December

	1999	2000	2001	2002	Total
Depreciation	4,000	4,000	4,000	4,000	16,000

The picture in the balance sheet will be:

Balance sheet extracts – at December 31

	1999	2000	2001	2002
Fixed asset – cost	20,000	20,000	20,000	20,000
Less: depreciation to date	4,000	8,000	12,000	16,000
Net book value	16,000	12,000	8,000	4,000

The reducing balance method

An alternative to the straight line method of depreciation is the reducing balance method, which charges more depreciation in the early years than in the later years of the asset's life. The calculation is made by applying a fixed percentage to the net brought forward figure (ie original cost less accumulated depreciation from previous years). The fixed percentage is derived from a mathematical formula.

EXAMPLE

Taking the same figures as in the above example, the result of the formula – the fixed percentage applied to the brought forward figure – is 33%. The application of the reducing balance method produces the following pattern of charges in the profit and loss account:

Profit and loss account extracts – for years ended December 31

	1999	2000	2001	2002	Total
Depreciation	6,600	4,422	2,963	1,985	15,970

The picture in the balance sheet will be:

Balance sheet extracts – at December 31				
	1999	2000	2001	2002
Fixed asset – cost	20,000	20,000	20,000	20,000
Less: depreciation to date	6,600	11,022	13,985	15,970
Net book value	13,400	8,978	6,015	4,030

Using this method the net book value at the end of the expected life of the asset will be close to, but will never exactly reach, the scrap value. This is due not only to the rounding to the nearest whole percentage point, but also to the mathematical relationship: taking a fixed percentage of an ever declining amount will never exactly reach zero.

Subjectivity in accounting

The choice of accounting method is an example of how accounting measurements are subjective rather than objective or scientifically precise. Essentially, accounting is more of an art than a science. The choice of which method to use is left entirely to the management, although the accounting methods chosen are expected to be appropriate to reflect the circumstances and conditions of the business, and should be applied consistently year on year to avoid distorting the trend of information. The choice between straight line and reducing balance methods can produce significantly different patterns of charges to the profit and loss account and also a different picture presented by the balance sheet at year ends, although over the long term these differences even out.

Additional elements of subjectivity are inherent in the calculation of depreciation. First, at the outset the expected useful life will have to be estimated. It is unlikely that this estimate will be absolutely accurate; the end of the asset's life may come sooner than expected, in which case insufficient amounts will have been written off for depreciation in prior periods. A loss on disposal will result, since sale proceeds are likely to be less than the net book value. Alternatively, the asset may have been written off too quickly, in which case the company may still be using working assets, even though these are not shown in the accounts.

Furthermore, the estimate of the eventual scrap value is subject to error, again raising the likelihood that there will be a difference between net book value and proceeds from the sale of the asset at the end of its life. Profits and losses on disposal of fixed assets should be treated through the profit and loss account and shown separately if they are material amounts.

Full disclosure of the chosen accounting methods will enable users of the accounts to see how the accounting figures have been calculated. In practice, disclosure tends to be restricted to a brief description of the method and the expected life or depreciation rate applied to assets.

ACCRUALS

Accruals is the term given for the adjustment required to reflect the benefit of goods and services received, but not yet paid for, in the accounting period. Thus, if an electricity bill of £2,000 for the quarter to 31 December 2001 is received in January 2002 and is not paid until February 2002, the profit and loss account should still bear the charge for the £2,000, since the benefit was consumed in that period. The balance sheet should include a credit of £2,000 – since this is the amount owing at 31 December 2001 for services received but not paid for. The adjustment is by double-entry:

> Debit: Electricity account (expense in the profit and loss account) £2,000
>
> Credit: Creditors account (accruals in the balance sheet) £2,000

Of course, goods and services may be paid for in advance (for example, insurance premiums and rent). This means that part (or all) of an item of expense paid for and recorded in the current period actually relates to a future accounting period. Again (as with stock), it would not be fair to charge the whole of such an expense item against the revenue of the period in which it was incurred; instead, it should be treated as a cost of the period to which it relates and which is expected to benefit from the goods or services.

Prepayments

Allowing for the prepayment is best dealt with through a post-trial balance adjustment. The effect of the adjustment is to reduce the expense item (ie credit the expense item) and to increase the assets (debit the balance sheet).

EXAMPLE

If a trader pays rent of £5,000 on premises for six months from 1 October 2001 and the accounting year end is 31 December 2001, it would be wrong to charge the whole £5,000 as an expense for the current period. The charge needs to be split between the relevant accounting periods which receive the benefit. This adjustment can be effected at the post-trial balance stage:

> Debit: Prepayment account (to be shown in the balance sheet as a current asset of £2,500);
>
> Credit: Rent account, £2,500.

BAD DEBTS

When it becomes clear that a debt is irrecoverable because, for example, the client has been declared bankrupt, it is necessary to write off the debt.

EXAMPLE

On 1 March 2002, a bill for fees of £1,500 was delivered to Worthless, a client. The double-entry is:

WORTHLESS ACCOUNT				
Date	Detail	DR	CR	Balance
1.3.02	Fees	1,500		1,500 DR

FEES ACCOUNT				
Date	Detail	DR	CR	Balance
1.3.02	Worthless		1,500	1,500 CR

On 1 June 2002, Worthless is declared bankrupt and the partners agree to write off the debt, since they realise that it is not acceptable to leave the balance as an asset.

The debt is cancelled by crediting the ledger account for that client account and debiting a bad debts account. At the end of the accounting period the balance on the bad debts account will be treated as another expense of trading and will be charged against the profit of the period. Note that a complete reversal of the original entries would have resulted in a debit to the fees account; however, this was not done because it is more useful to keep a separate account for the amount of debts written off.

WORTHLESS ACCOUNT				
Date	Detail	DR	CR	Balance
1.3.02	Fees	1,500		1,500 DR
1.6.02	Bad debts account		1,500	0

BAD DEBTS ACCOUNT				
Date	Detail	DR	CR	Balance
1.6.02	Worthless	1,500		1,500 DR

VAT can be reclaimed on a debt which has not been received within six months of the date of the bill, provided that the VAT has been paid to the Customs and Excise and that the debt has been written off for accounting purposes.

Specific and general provisions for bad debts

It is not always possible to state that a debt is irrecoverable with complete finality. However, there may be indications that specific debts are likely to be irrecoverable. In addition, experience suggests that other unidentified clients may suffer from financial difficulties and be unable to pay their debts.

In these circumstances, it is a prudent policy to make provision for the likelihood of specific debts being bad and to estimate others becoming irrecoverable. These provisions are known as 'specific' and 'general' respectively. Specific bad debt provisions are allowable for tax purposes but general provisions are not tax deductible.

The accounting for provisions is not as complicated as it may at first seem. To set up a provision the double-entry is:

> DEBIT   the bad debts account and
> CREDIT a provision for doubtful debts account

Debts which go bad during the year will be written off as they occur. If a specific provision has already been made for a debt which subsequently proves to be irrecoverable then the debt will be written off against the provision:

> DEBIT   the provision account for that specific doubtful debt (to eliminate the provision)
> CREDIT the individual debtor's account (to eliminate the debt)

In subsequent years, the provisions will have to be reviewed in the light of debts existing at each balance sheet date. The charge against profit will only be for any further increase in the provisions which might be deemed necessary. Of course, if the existing provisions are deemed to be excessive, then they will be reduced by writing back the excess to the profit and loss account.

Businesses must regularly review the state of their debtors to identify those which may prove difficult or impossible to recover. Such a review might include:

- examination of the composition and age of every debtor balance;
- if a debt has been outstanding for some time, ascertaining what if any steps to obtain settlement have been taken;
- writing off known bad debts;
- making provision for those debtors which seem likely to be irrecoverable; and
- providing for unknown bad debts (ie make a general provision).

EXAMPLE

At 31 October 2001, Johnson & Co extracted a list of its debtor balances which totalled £126,000. Included in the list were the following debtors:

- Balzac, who owed £2,000 but was now known to be bankrupt,
- Evans, who owed £4,000 but was known to be in financial difficulties.

The partners of Johnson & Co agree that it would be prudent to write off Balzac's debt and to make a provision against the debt of Evans. In addition, from past experience, they consider that they require a general provision for doubtful debts equivalent to 2% of the debtor balances, excluding those which are subject to a specific provision.

The double-entry for the first of these three treatments is:

	Account	Amount	Journal entry
DR	Bad debts account		Being bad debt written off
		£2,000	
CR	Balzac account		

The double-entry to record the creation of the specific provision for Evans' debt is:

	Account	Amount	Journal entry
DR	Bad debts account		
		£4,000	Being provision against Evans' debt
CR	Specific provision for doubtful debt account (Evans)		

The double-entry to record the creation of the general provision of 2% against other possible doubtful debts is:

	Account	Amount	Journal entry
DR	Bad debts account		
		£2,400	Being establishment of general provision equal to 2% of debtor balances
CR	Specific provision for doubtful debt account		

The balance on the bad debts account will end up in the profit and loss account as a charge or expense of £8,400 (£2,000 + £4,000 + £2,400).

The balance sheet presentation will appear as:

Debtors*	124,000
Less: Provision for Doubtful Debts	(6,400)
	117,600

* After writing off the bad debt.

During the year to 31 October 2002, all the end of 2001 balances (excluding the debts of Balzac and Evans) were settled in full. Evans was declared bankrupt and the debt showing on his ledger account was written off against the specific provision. Any other bad debts would be written off as they occurred during the year.

EXAMPLE

At 31 October 2002, the total of the balances on the ledger accounts for client matters in the books of Johnson & Co came to £150,000. These balances include one client, Phillips, whose debt of £5,000 has been outstanding for six months and who has failed to respond to a final reminder and a threat of legal action for recovery of the debt. The policy of providing for 2% of the outstanding balances is to be continued. In preparing the final accounts for the year ended 31 October 2002, the first thing to do is to write off any known bad debts included in the £150,000. Assuming there are none, the next stage is to identify specific debts which are doubtful, in this case, Phillips. Assuming that this is the only debtor to appear doubtful the final stage is to adjust the general provision for doubtful debts so that it reflects the firm's policy. Thus:

	Account	Amount	Journal entry
DR	Bad debts account	£5,000	Being provision against Phillips debt
CR	Specific provision for doubtful debts account		

and

	Account	Amount	Journal entry
DR	Bad debts account	£500	Being necessary increase in provision
CR	General provision for doubtful debts account		

In addition to the specific provisions needed to be established against debts at the year end, the profit and loss account will be charged with any difference between the general provision brought forward from last year and the general provision required at the end of the current year. The general provision will be 'topped up' to £2,900 by a further charge to the profit and loss account of £500; if a reduction in the provision is required, this will result in a credit to the profit and loss account.

CONCLUSION

This chapter has introduced the major types of post-trial balance adjustments. In practice, such adjustments are required to achieve a fair matching of costs and revenues through the application of the matching or accruals concept. The variety of real world examples of accruals is endless, and will reflect on the type and nature of the business. Nevertheless, the accounting treatment will follow the same principles. If the business has received the benefit in any one accounting year, the profit and loss account should bear the cost; if the benefit has not been paid for, the business must have a liability. The double-entry for such adjustments may not appear to be straightforward, but it is part of the attempt to ensure that the financial statements accurately portray the progress and position of a business.

EXERCISES

1. The trial balance for Ruddock shows:

	DR	CR
	£	£
Sales		94,000
Purchases	64,000	
Operating expenses	5,000	
Selling expenses	1,000	
Plant	30,000	
Drawings	5,000	
Cash	4,000	
Capital		15,000
Total	109,000	109,000

The closing stock is £5,000.

Prepare the final accounts, ie profit and loss account and the balance sheet.

2. Olivia is in business selling jewellery and the trial balance at the end of the year is:

	DR	CR
	£	£
Sales		46,000
Debtors	500	
Opening stock	6,000	
Purchases	15,000	
Rent	1,500	
Wages	1,000	
Fixtures	28,000	
Capital account		25,000
Drawings account	19,000	
	71,000	71,000

The following adjustments are required to be made:

(a) A depreciation charge of £7,000 for wear and tear on the fixtures.
(b) Closing stock costing £5,000.
(c) Rates for the last year of £10,000 have not yet been paid.

Prepare the Profit and Loss Account and Balance Sheet.

3. Leigh is a trader who extracts the following balances from the books at the end of the trading year on 31 March 2002:

	DR	CR
	£	£
Sales		100,000
Purchases	50,000	
Expenses	15,000	
Stock at 1.4.01	1,000	
Plant	10,000	
Capital account		10,000
Debtors	24,000	
Cash at bank	10,000	
	110,000	110,000

You note that no entries have been made to allow for the following:

(a) Stock unsold at 31 March 2002 cost £5,000.
(b) Depreciation of 25% pa is to be charged on the cost of the plant.
(c) Debts amounting to £1,000 appear to be irrecoverable.
(d) Of the £15,000 paid for expenses, £2,000 relates to the year ended 31 March 2003.

Prepare the final accounts for the year ended 31 March 2002.

4. A trial balance for an architect, a sole practitioner, for the year ending 31 December 2001 is as follows:

	DR	CR
	£	£
Your capital account		35,000
Retained profit		4,740
Fees		60,000
Drawings	9,600	
Work-in-progress (1.1.01)	5,000	
Rent	1,200	
Rates	530	
Stationery	640	
Wages	20,520	
Car expenses	4,800	
Fixtures (bought 1.1.00)	50,000	
Provision for depreciation at 1.1.01		12,500
Cash at bank	10,000	
Debtors	10,000	
General provision for doubtful debts at 1.1.01		50
	112,290	112,290

You discover that no entries have been made to reflect the following conditions:

(a) The item 'car expenses' includes the insurance premium for 2002 of £1,000.

(b) Work-in-progress at 31 December 2001 costs £15,000.

(c) Straight line depreciation of 25% is to be charged on the cost of the fixtures for 2001.

(d) The writing off of a £500 bad debt.

(e) The general provision for doubtful debts is to be increased to £95.

Prepare an income and expenditure account for the year ended 31 December 2001 and a balance sheet at 31 December 2001.

Chapter 13

Analysis and interpretation of accounts

INTRODUCTION

The previous chapters have attempted to explain how accounting records are maintained and how the data recorded in ledger accounts are transformed into information in the form of final accounts, the profit and loss account and balance sheet. To be able to interpret the information contained in financial statements is a valuable skill, which professional people are increasingly expected to possess.

This chapter begins with a general overview of the environment which governs the preparation of financial statements before moving on to consider the basic and fundamental accounting concepts which underpin financial statements. It is important to have an understanding of these concepts before tackling the issue of analysis and interpretation.

THE REGULATORY ENVIRONMENT

Accounting by limited companies is governed by both the provisions of the Companies Act 1985, as amended by the Companies Act 1989, and the accounting 'rules' developed by the Accounting Standards Board (ASB). The ASB issues Financial Reporting Standards (FRSs) and has adopted the Statements of Standard Accounting Practice (SSAPs) from a predecessor body. The FRSs and SSAPs apply to any financial statements intended to give 'a true and fair view', but they are also adopted by many other concerns and it is clear that the ASB has as its aim the improvement of financial reporting in general.

To assist the ASB in producing authoritative guidance on a timely basis, the Urgent Issues Task Force issues 'Abstracts' which, though lacking the authority of FRSs and SSAPs, are nevertheless regarded as part of the body of accepted practices determining what constitutes a 'true and fair view'.

The ASB is guided by the Financial Reporting Council, whose members represent various sectional interests such as government, the City, industry and the accounting profession. Apparent breaches of the accounting rules may be inquired into by the Review Panel, which has the authority to apply to the court for a declaration that a set of accounts does not comply with statutory requirements and for an order requiring the directors to revise the company's financial statements. The Review Panel has persuaded a number of companies to amend their financial statements and accounting procedures without having to go to court.

The ASB is not the only regulator producing pronouncements on how financial information is produced and presented. There is an International Accounting Standards Board (IASB) which produces International Financial Reporting Standards (IFRSs). The IASB has become very influential and national standard-setting bodies, like the ASB in the Untied Kingdom, are under increasing pressure to ensure that their national standards are aligned with the IFRSs. For example, the European Commission has stated that financial statements of companies listed in the European Union should comply with the IFRSs by 2005.

ACCOUNTING PRINCIPLES

The ASB has issued a 'Statement of Principles for Financial Reporting', which is the conceptual basis for the preparation of financial statements. This statement follows substantially the IASB's 'Framework for the Preparation and Presentation of Financial Statements' so one can be sure that the main ideas espoused therein are internationally accepted.

The statement begins with a discussion of the need for financial statements and asserts that information is useful for economic decision-making. It then identifies parties who might have an interest in financial statements, such as present and potential investors, lenders, trade suppliers, employees, customers, government agencies and the general public. Finally, the statement identifies desirable characteristics which would make financial information useful.

Relevance

Clearly, if information is to be useful it must be relevant to users' decisions and be presented in time to influence their decisions. Relevant information either assists users in assessing past, present or future events or confirms users' past assessments. There are different perspectives from which users may view an entity, but the one which is most relevant is based on the assumption that the entity is going to continue into the foreseeable future. This has long been referred to as the going concern concept or assumption. This assumption allows assets to be recorded at cost or written down values rather than the values those assets might attract in the event of liquidation.

Reliability

To be useful, information must be reliable. Reliable information faithfully represents the transactions and events which have occurred and is presented in a neutral way, without bias. Another, perhaps obvious, quality is that reliable information contains no *material* errors. The information must also be complete, that is, there should be no material omissions, for example, undisclosed liabilities. Finally, prudence is to be used when dealing with uncertainties, for example, regarding asset values. The application of prudence means that profits are not recognised until they are realised, whereas unrealised losses may be recognised. For example, it is prudent to value stock and work-in-progress at the lower of cost and net realisable value (NRV – which is the anticipated sales price, less any additional costs which would need to be incurred in selling the stock). By taking the lower of the two valuations, profit will never be overstated because:

- where the NRV of the stock exceeds its cost, stock is valued at cost to avoid anticipating the unrealised profit, the profit on the future sale of the stock;
- where NRV is below cost, stock is valued at NRV to recognise the anticipated loss.

However, the exercise of prudence should not be used to justify the deliberate under-valuing of assets and/or the over-valuing of liabilities, since this would introduce bias and would distort the view given by the financial statements.

Comparability

The next quality is that of comparability. There are very few situations where users of accounting information would be interested in a single set of financial statements in isolation. In most cases, users will want to see at least one other period's statements or the statements of at least one other entity so that some comparisons can be made: is the entity doing as well this year as last? Or, is it doing as well as a competitor or rival organisation? Such comparisons would be meaningless if, unknown to the users, the information being used for comparative purposes were drawn up on completely different bases. Thus there is a need for *consistency*. Directors should choose the most appropriate accounting policies designed to produce a true and fair view. These policies should be consistently applied year on year, for example, the same method of depreciating fixed assets should be used year after year unless there is good reason to change. In the event of a change of policy, the directors are expected to disclose the fact that there has been a change in policy, to give an explanation of the reason for the change and, if possible, an estimate of the effect of the change.

However, different companies may have legitimate reasons for choosing different policies; there is no requirement that there be absolute uniformity between companies since each is in many ways unique. However, in order to enable users to be able to compare different companies' reports, there is a need for adequate disclosure of the major accounting policies adopted (see FRS 18, Accounting Policies). Such disclosure allows users to make appropriate adjustments to accounting information so that meaningful inter-company comparisons can be made.

Understandability

The final quality is understandability. To be useful and useable information must be understandable. Data must be clearly presented in a manner that conveys the substance of what has happened. Users' understanding is clearly a function of their knowledge and abilities, and preparers of financial information are entitled to assume that the users of the information have a reasonable grasp of business activities and a willingness to use reasonable diligence in analysing the information. Tied to understandability is the concept of materiality.

Materiality

Materiality is a threshold quality similar to the legal principle of de minimis. Financial statements are summaries of all the details recorded in the ledger accounts and other accounting records. Since it is impossible for all the details to be represented, those responsible for the preparation of the financial statements must decide how much information should be disclosed. Too little information and the reader will not have sufficient data to enable a fair assessment to be made; too much information and the reader will not be able to see the wood for the trees. Considered judgments are required to determine those items which should be shown separately and those which may be aggregated. The test of materiality is whether the separate disclosure of an item would affect the view given by the financial statements. This is a highly subjective area of accounting, for which no hard and fast rules exist.

In addition to the going concern concept referred to above, FRS 18 identifies a second concept which has a pervasive effect on financial statements: the accruals concept. The accruals concept seeks to ensure that transactions are recorded in the correct accounting period, the period in which they have occurred not the period in which cash is received or paid. Thus, year end adjustments are made to record expenses which have been incurred in one period but will not be paid until the next period.

Limitations of financial statements

Students should be aware that there are limitations to the accountants' art.

Money measurement

The ledger accounts, and hence the financial statements, show only the effects of business transactions which have been expressed in monetary amounts. Non-monetary effects, such as customer loyalty and the expertise and motivation of employees, while undoubtedly of value to the business, cannot be measured in monetary terms and so cannot be reflected in the financial statements.

Historical cost

Since the ledger accounts record past transactions, assets generally appear in the financial statements at their original cost less any amounts written off. These 'book values' will almost certainly vary from current market values or forced sale values. It is therefore a serious mistake to view the balance sheet as a measure of the business's value.

COMPANY FINANCIAL STATEMENTS

Share capital

There are several terms associated with share capital of which the reader should be aware:

Nominal capital

A company issues shares of a 'nominal' value, ie face value. For example, many small companies have a nominal capital of 100 £1 ordinary shares.

Authorised capital

The term 'authorised capital' refers to the maximum number of shares the company is authorised to issue by its memorandum of association.

Issued capital

Issued capital refers to the amount of shares which have been issued, which obviously should not exceed the authorised limit.

Paid-up capital

Paid-up capital refers to the extent to which subscribers have paid the issue price. Shares can be issued as fully paid or partly paid, although, in the latter case, the shareholder continues to be liable for the unpaid balance of the issue price.

Share premium

Shares may be issued at a 'premium' – that is, the issue price of the shares is above the nominal value. A share premium must be separately accounted for. It is contrary to company law to issue shares at a discount.

Market value

Once issued, the shares in quoted companies are subsequently traded at prices which are determined by the market forces of supply and demand. These market prices may be vastly different from the nominal value of the shares.

Ordinary versus preference shares

Preference shares have priority over ordinary shares in terms of the right to a dividend and repayment of capital before the holders of ordinary shares.

Ordinary shares can be sold to new buyers but can only be redeemed by the company under certain circumstances. Thus, ordinary shares are seen as the permanent capital of the business.

Dividends

The returns to shareholders are in the form of dividends which are distributions of profits not expenses against profits.

Debentures

Debentures are loans to the company commanding both interest payment (which is an expense against profit) and usually a right to repayment of the principal.

The purpose of interpreting financial statements

The extent of an examination of a set of accounts will depend on the purpose of such an examination. A solicitor may be required to act for a variety of potential users of a set of financial statements, for example:

- A potential investor may wish to judge whether a business is a sound investment.
- The existing owner may want to compare results with the results of other similar businesses or may be in the process of negotiating the sale of the business.
- A creditor may want to consider the risk of lending to the business.
- Employees may want representation in pay negotiations.
- A client may need advice in relation to tax returns or an application for government grants.

Considering financial statements

The basic steps when considering financial statements are:

- Determine the ability and standing of the person preparing the financial statements.
- Obtain financial statements for a number of years in order to determine trends and eliminate unusual situations.
- Establish whether the trade is seasonal or is affected by any other factors which might distort the picture given by the financial statements.
- Check whether the financial statements contain any valuations and, if so, the competence and independence of the valuer.
- Inquire into any reported aggregate figure and if possible obtain more detailed analyses of the total (for example, a debtors ageing analysis).

Basic principles of interpretation

If we are comparing two competing traders, simply looking at the absolute figures will give only limited information.

EXAMPLE

	Trader A	Trader B
Sales	100,000	10,000
Cost of sales	50,000	6,000
Gross profit	50,000	4,000

The basic information we can see is that:

- Sales in A are ten times greater than in B.
- Trader A makes a gross profit of £50,000, whereas Trader B makes a profit of £4,000.

By converting the *absolute* amounts of gross profit into percentages of sales, we are better able to assess the *relative* profitability of the two traders. Trader A has made a 50% gross profit, whereas Trader B can only manage 40%. This observation prompts the question: Why? The financial statements may not provide all the answers, but an analysis of the statements may provide the structure for a more detailed investigation. For instance, in the above example, it may be found that Trader A, being larger, can negotiate better purchase prices with suppliers, perhaps taking advantage of bulk discounts.

The key to this type of analysis is *comparison* – the results must be compared with something, whether that be previous years' results, projected results, competitors' results or industry norms.

Efficiency and effectiveness ratios

Efficiency and effectiveness ratios focus on the sales and profit figures in relation to other items in the financial statements.

Gross profit percentage (margin or mark-up)

Gross profit is a very important factor in any trader's business. Gross profit is the difference between the value of items sold and the purchase cost of those items. If the gross profit is insufficient to cover the other, overhead expenses, the trader will report a net loss.

Gross profit may be expressed as a percentage of sales:

$$\text{Gross profit margin} \quad \frac{\text{Gross profit}}{\text{Sales}} \times 100$$

Alternatively, gross profit may be expressed as a percentage of the cost of sales (known as the 'mark-up' on cost):

$$\text{Gross profit mark-up} \quad \frac{\text{Gross profit}}{\text{Cost of sales}} \times 100$$

In practice, the gross profit percent varies between types of traders. Some products have a low gross profit percentage but a very high volume of sales; others have a high gross profit percentage and a low volume of sales. It is therefore essential to compare like with like. However, for an individual business the gross profit percentage is a key indicator because it measures the profit on trading (ie the difference between buying costs and selling values). Fluctuations in the gross margin need to be investigated. A decrease in the margin may indicate theft of the stock or under-recording of sales. An increase in the margin may result from inadvertent errors or deliberate manipulation; for example, purchase invoices may have been overlooked or deliberately suppressed or the closing stock figure may have been overstated.

Net profit margin

An important measure of profitability is the net profit margin, which shows how much profit is made on the turnover after all expenses have been deducted:

$$\text{Net profit percentage} \quad \frac{\text{Net profit}}{\text{Sales}} \quad \times 100$$

Return on capital employed

The net profit figure also needs to be related to the investment required to earn the profit. One difficulty with ratios involving capital employed is the variety of definitions of capital employed. Possible definitions include total assets, net assets and long-term funds (ie debt and equity). For the purposes of analysis, any definition is acceptable provided it is used consistently.

This produces a rate of return which can be used as a comparison with other forms of investment:

$$\text{Return on capital employed} \quad \frac{\text{Net profit}}{\text{Net assets}} \quad \times 100$$

An alternative definition of capital employed uses total assets as the denominator, ie this disregards the source of funds (whether long-term, debt or equity, or short-term creditors).

$$\text{Return on capital employed} \quad \frac{\text{Net profit}}{\text{Total assets}} \quad \times 100$$

Effectiveness ratio

In addition to discovering the profitability or efficiency of a business, readers should be interested in how effectively the assets have been employed in generating revenue:

$$\text{Effectiveness ratio} \quad \frac{\text{Sales}}{\text{Capital employed}}$$

This is a 'pure' ratio, not a percentage. It measures the relationship between sales and net assets (again, there are various definitions of capital employed).

The significance of this ratio is that a business with net assets of £1m making sales of £5m (effectiveness ratio of 5:1) is not as effective in using its assets to generate turnover as a business with net assets of £10,000 which produces sales of £100,000 (a ratio of 10:1).

Working capital management

One factor frequently overlooked by entrepreneurs is that, even if they have a highly profitable business with substantial assets, the risk of insolvency is still present. Businesses fail not because they make losses but because they are unable to settle their debts as they fall due. To reduce the risk of failure, businesses therefore need to have adequate resources in the form of liquid assets, ie either cash or things that can be turned into cash in the short term. One measure used to assess this is the current ratio:

$$\text{Current ratio} \quad \frac{\text{Current assets}}{\text{Current liabilities}}$$

As a rule of thumb, this ratio ought not to be less than 2:1, although this depends on the industry and other factors, such as the profit margin on the stock or work-in-progress. To provide a margin of safety, a variant of the working capital ratio excludes stock from the current assets, ie the ratio is:

$$[\text{debtors and cash : current liabilities}]$$

The reason for the omission of stock/work-in-progress from the ratio is that this is usually the least liquid of the current assets. This ratio is known as the liquidity or 'acid test' ratio:

$$\text{Liquidity ratio} \quad \frac{\text{Liquid assets}}{\text{Current liabilities}}$$

Some idea of the effectiveness of the management of working capital can be obtained by looking at the 'turnover' of the various components of working capital; for example, the length of time a business takes to collect its debts. It should be remembered that, to the extent that debtors take credit, the business is financing its customers. We can determine the average collection period of debtors by calculating the debtors' turnover ratio:

$$\text{Debtors' turnover ratio} \quad \frac{\text{Sales}}{\text{Debtors}}$$

$$\text{Expressed in days} \quad \frac{365}{\text{Ratio}}$$

For example, a company has annual sales of £1,200,000 and average debtors of £300,000. The debtors' turnover ratio is therefore:

$$\frac{£1,200,000}{£300,000} = 4 \text{ times}$$

Expressed in days $\qquad \dfrac{365}{4} = 91 \text{ days}$

On the opposite side of the coin, the creditors of a business provide it with finance. The creditors' payment period measures the speed with which creditors are paid:

Creditors turnover ratio $\qquad \dfrac{\text{Purchases}}{\text{Creditors}}$

Expressed in days $\qquad \dfrac{365}{\text{Ratio}}$

For example, a company has annual purchases of £600,000 and average creditors of £100,000:

$$\frac{£600,000}{£100,000} = 6 \text{ times}$$

Expressed in days $\qquad \dfrac{365}{6} = 61 \text{ days}$

In addition, another critical aspect of working capital management is the stock holding period. The 'stock turnover ratio' determines the length of time the average item stays in stock:

Stock turnover ratio $\qquad \dfrac{\text{Cost of sales}}{\text{Average stock}}$

Expressed in days $\qquad \dfrac{365}{\text{Ratio}}$

For example, a company's annual cost of sales is £500,000 and it has average stock of £100,000:

$$\frac{£500,000}{£100,000} = 5$$

Expressed in days $\quad \dfrac{365}{5} = 73 \text{ days}$

It is usual for the rate of stock turnover to be higher in the case of cheap items and lower for large expensive items. Nevertheless, all businesses seek a high rate of stock turnover, as this reduces stock holding costs such as storage and the risk of obsolescence.

From these three working capital management ratios, we can calculate the cash operating cycle, which is the period from the receipt of goods to the final collection of cash from sales. It is measured by adding the stock-holding period to the debtors' collection period and deducting the creditors' payment period.

We should, of course, be careful in interpreting the results of these ratios, since the transactions reported in the profit and loss account may not have accrued evenly over the year and the year end balances may not be representative of the position of the business at other times during the year.

Gearing

'Gearing' is a term which is used to compare the amount of finance borrowed with the amount of finance provided by the owner (or shareholders). The gearing ratio is calculated as:

$$\text{Gearing} \quad \frac{\text{Amount borrowed}}{\text{Total long-term funds}} \quad \times 100$$

A business relying too heavily on borrowed funds is said to be 'overgeared'.

Note that whenever a ratio involves a balance sheet figure, it should strictly be an average of opening and closing balance sheets, since this is likely to be more accurate.

Market ratios

In the context of a quoted company, one ratio that investment analysts are concerned with is the 'earnings per share' (EPS). In simple terms, the EPS is the company's net profit divided by the number of shares in issue. Thus:

$$\text{Earnings per share (EPS)} \quad \frac{\text{Net profit}}{\text{No of ordinary shares}}$$

By itself the EPS contains little information but, when it is related to the price of a share in the relevant company, it forms a key stock market performance indicator.

$$\text{Price earnings (PE) ratio} \quad \frac{\text{Market price per share}}{\text{Earnings per share}}$$

A high PE ratio reflects the market's confidence in the future prospects of the company concerned.

But investors are also concerned with the security of their present income from holding shares, that is, their income from dividends. A measure of the safety of the dividend payout ratio is provided by the dividend cover:

$$\text{Dividend cover} \quad \frac{\text{Earnings per share}}{\text{Dividend per share}}$$

The dividend cover ratio measures the risk of a fall in dividends, in terms of how far profits have to fall before threatening the current level of dividends. The higher the ratio the more secure the dividend.

In order to compare various forms of investment opportunities, the wise investor needs to know the rate of return which each investment provides. The dividend yield attempts to provide an indication of future returns by expressing the latest dividend as a percentage of the current share price.

$$\text{Dividend yield} \quad \frac{\text{Gross dividend}}{\text{Market price per share}}$$

Further insight into the financial management of a business can be obtained by reviewing the cash flow statement where this is presented.

CONCLUSION

This chapter has provided a brief overview of the regulatory environment of financial reporting, of particular issues affecting limited companies, and of various methods of analysing financial statements.

In the context of the latter issue, it is appropriate to conclude with a few words of caution:

■ A single year's figures are unlikely to be sufficient for a proper investigation. The general trend and progress of the business can be assessed only by obtaining several years' figures.

■ The financial statements reflect only transactions that are measured in financial terms. There may be assets which are not capable of monetary measurement (for example, the loyalty of customers or the morale of the work force).

■ The financial statements are historical by nature and are only a guide to future results.

■ The financial statements may be distorted by unusual events or transactions.

■ Accounting is not a precise science. There are numerous areas where the exercise of judgment is required, for example, the range of possible depreciation rates and methods. Without full disclosure of the accounting policies used in preparing a set of financial statements, it may be difficult to judge the picture portrayed by the statements.

EXERCISES

1. Identify different uses and users of financial statements.

2. Identify the key characteristics which are needed if financial information is to be considered useful.

3. Who issues accounting standards and how are they enforced?

4. Explain the limitations of the conventional bases on which financial statements are prepared.

5. The accounts of Turk Ltd and Jackie Ltd for the year ended 31 March 2002 are shown below:

Profit and loss accounts				
	Turk		*Jackie*	
Sales		50,000		100,000
Less:				
Opening stock	10,000		12,000	
Purchases	35,000		77,000	
Closing stock	(10,000)		(15,000)	
Cost of sales		(35,000)		(74,000)
Gross profit		15,000		26,000
Expenses		(11,000)		(17,000)
Net profit		4,000		9,000

Balance sheets				
	Turk		Jackie	
	£	£	£	£
Fixed assets:				
Buildings	7,000		11,000	
Fixtures	1,500		4,000	
		8,500		15,000
Current assets				
Stock	10,000		15,000	
Debtors	9,500		15,000	
Bank	5,500		–	
	25,000		30,000	
Less: current liabilities				
Creditors	7,000		16,000	
Bank	–		500	
Net current assets		18,000		13,500
		26,500		28,500
Less: debentures		10,000		–
Net assets		16,500		28,500
Financed by:				
£1 ordinary shares		5,000		10,000
Retained profit		11,500		18,500
		16,500		28,500

Prepare a report for the directors of Turk Ltd, in which you compare the position and performance of the two companies supporting your analysis with relevant accounting ratios.

6. Bird & Co is a partnership of solicitors. The firm's financial statements are:

PROFIT AND LOSS ACCOUNT FOR THE YEAR ENDED ON 31 MAY				
	2002		2001	
	£000	£000	£000	£000
INCOME				
Bills delivered		1,654		1,520
Interest and commissions		30		25
		1,684		1,545
LESS: EXPENSES				
STAFF				
Salaried partners	215		193	
Assistant solicitors	101		70	
Legal executives	135		124	
Articled clerks	25		15	
Typists	286		232	
Accounts/cashiers	27		44	
Other administration	36		33	
	825		711	
ACCOMMODATION				
Rent	55		55	
Rates	20		18	
Heat and light	20		17	
Repairs and maintenance	27		28	
	122		118	
OTHER				
Library, stationery, postage	86		81	
Travel	46		43	
Telephone	39		36	
Insurance	44		42	
Miscellaneous	93		96	
	308		298	
NON-CASH EXPENSES				
Bad debts	25		7	
Depreciation on equipment and vehicles	76		71	
Decrease in work-in-progress	8		0	
	109		78	
TOTAL EXPENSES		1,364		1,205
NET OPERATING PROFIT		320		340

BALANCE SHEET AS AT 31 MAY				
	2002		2001	
	£000	£000	£000	£000
FIXED ASSETS				
Leasehold improvements	50		15	
Computer	35		30	
Furniture and equipment	82		114	
Vehicles	120	287	90	249
CURRENT ASSETS				
Work-in-progress	408		416	
Debtors	381		333	
Cash	25		46	
	814		795	
LESS				
CURRENT LIABILITIES				
Creditors	112		98	
Bank overdraft	410		350	
	522		448	
WORKING CAPITAL		292		347
NET ASSETS EMPLOYED		579		596
Financed by:				
Partners' capital accounts		480		480
Partners' current accounts		99		116
NET CAPITAL EMPLOYED		579		596

Prepare an analysis of the performance and position of Bird & Co.

Note

Exercise 6 is based on the Best Practice kit published by (and reproduced by kind permission of) the Law Society for England and Wales.

Chapter 14

More advanced aspects of accounting

INTRODUCTION

In practice there are numerous areas of technical difficulties in financial reporting. This chapter looks at two advanced aspects of accounting: accounting for groups and the treatment of taxation. We have considered it appropriate to give only a brief insight into these two topics, the immense complexities of which are deserving of an entire textbook in their own right.

ACCOUNTING FOR GROUPS

A group of companies consists of a main company (known as a holding or parent company) and one or more other companies, controlled by the holding company (known as subsidiary companies).

Definition of a subsidiary company

A company (H Ltd) is a parent company of another company (S Ltd) if it:

■ owns a majority of the voting rights in S Ltd;

■ is a member of S Ltd and has the right to appoint or remove a majority of its board of directors;

■ has the right to exercise a dominant influence over S Ltd by virtue of S Ltd's memorandum or articles or a control contract; or

■ is a member of S Ltd and controls alone a majority of the voting rights in S Ltd.

In the balance sheet of the holding company the cost of purchasing the shares will generally be shown as an asset. Each company is required to maintain its own accounting records and prepare its own financial statements. Holding companies must also prepare consolidated financial statements for the group as if it were a single entity. The aim is to reduce the scope for fraudulent reporting by, for example, inter-company trading: the same goods could be traded back and forth at ever increasing prices creating purely fictitious profits.

Of course, the group is not a single entity for legal purposes: for example, contracts with suppliers or lenders will be made with the individual company concerned.

The procedure to prepare a consolidated balance sheet is:

■ Draw up the final accounts of the holding company and its subsidiary(ies).

■ Cancel out any items which are purely intra-group, for example, an asset in one company and a liability in another company.

■ Items which remain uncancelled are added together on a line-by-line basis, for example, sales in Company A is added to the sales in Company B, to produce a composite or aggregate picture for the group as a whole.

EXAMPLE

Major Ltd purchased all the shares in Minor Ltd at the start of the year for £4,000, which was a fair value for the assets acquired. The financial statements of the two companies at 31 December 2001 are:

Profit and Loss Accounts for the year ended 31 December 2001

	Major Ltd		Minor Ltd	
	£	£	£	£
Sales		500,000		100,000
Less: Cost of sales		400,000		50,000
Gross Profit		100,000		50,000
Dividends received		2,000		
Less: Overheads	50,000		30,000	
Management charge paid/(received)	(10,000)		10,000	
		40,000		40,000
Net profit		62,000		10,000
Less dividends paid		44,000		2,000
Retained profit		18,000		8,000

Balance Sheets at 31 December 2001

	Major Ltd		Minor Ltd	
	£	£	£	£
Fixed Assets		60,000		12,000
Shares in Minor Ltd		4,000		
Current Assets				
Stock	3,000		5,000	
Debtors			1,000	
Group debtor	5,000			
Cash	4,000			
	12,000		6,000	
Less:				
Creditors	8,000		1,000	
Group creditor			5,000	
	8,000		6,000	
Net current assets		4,000		0
Net assets		68,000		12,000
Financed by:				
£1 Ordinary Shares		50,000		4,000
Retained profits		18,000		8,000
		68,000		12,000

The first step is to identify any intra-group balances in both the profit and loss accounts and the balance sheets. In the profit and loss account, we can see that the dividend received shown by Major Ltd is matched by the dividend paid by Minor Ltd. Similarly the management charge which is income for Major Ltd is an expense for Minor Ltd. Both items are purely within the group, no third parties are involved and so no entries for these items should appear in the group accounts.

Looking at the balance sheet we see that there is a group debtor in the current assets of Major Ltd and a group creditor as a current liability of Minor Ltd. Also, there is the investment in the subsidiary shown as an asset in the parent company's balance sheet which is matched by the nominal value of the shares in the subsidiary's balance sheet; these shares are not held by members outside of the group and no third party is affected. Again, these are purely intra-group and should not appear in the group balance sheet.

Having cancelled out the intra-group balances the rest are added across to give the following group financial statements:

Group Profit and Loss Account for the year ended 31 December 2000

	£
Sales (500+100)	600,000
Less: Cost of sales (400+50)	450,000
Gross Profit	150,000
Dividends received	0
Less:	
Overheads (50+30)	80,000
Management charge paid/(received)	0
	80,000
Net profit	70,000
Less dividends paid	44,000
Retained profit	26,000

Group Balance Sheet at 31 December 2000

	£	£
Fixed Assets (60+12)		72,000
Shares in Minor Ltd		0
Current Assets		
Stock (3+5)	8,000	
Debtors	1,000	
Group debtor	0	
Cash	4,000	
	13,000	
Less:		
Creditors (8+1)	9,000	
Group creditor	0	
	9,000	
Net current assets		4,000
		76,000
Financed by:		
£1 Ordinary Shares		50,000
Retained profits		26,000
		76,000

Further complications

Difficulties arise when the cost of the shares in the subsidiary is not equal to the nominal value of the shares, ie the acquiring company was prepared to pay more than the nominal value of the shares acquired. Let us suppose instead that Major Ltd had paid £7,000 for all 4,000 £1 shares (and consequently its cash balance is £3,000 less, although all other balances are the same as in the example above). The problem now is that, in producing the consolidated accounts, the investment by Major Ltd in Minor Ltd will not be cancelled by the share capital of Minor Ltd: there will be a balance of £3,000 remaining. This is known as 'goodwill' and should be shown as an asset in the consolidated balance sheet (and like any other long-term asset, depreciated over its useful life although it is more correct to talk of *amortising* goodwill). The authoritative guidance for the accounting for goodwill and other intangible assets is to be found in FRS10.

The consolidated balance sheet at 31 December 2001 becomes:

	Group	
	£	£
Fixed assets		72,000
Goodwill		3,000
Current assets		
Stock	8,000	
Debtors	1,000	
Cash	1,000	
	10,000	
Less:		
Creditors	9,000	
	9,000	
		1,000
		76,000
Capital		
£1 ordinary shares		50,000
Retained profits		26,000
		76,000

Minority interests

If the holding company acquires less than 100% of the shares of the subsidiary, there is a minority interest in the subsidiary. Suppose, for example, that Major Ltd had paid £7,000 for only 3,000 £1 shares. This change of conditions has two effects: first the goodwill is now £4,000 (ie the difference between what Major Ltd paid and what it got). The second effect is that although we treat the group as controlling the subsidiary, the group must recognise that outsiders also have a stake in the profits and net assets of the subsidiary. In the group profit and loss account and balance sheet therefore recognition must be given to the claims of the minority shareholders who are entitled to be credited with their share of the profit for the year, share capital and retained profits of the subsidiary.

Group Profit and Loss Account for the year ended 31 December 2001

	£	£
Sales (500+100)		600,000
Less: (400+50)		450,000
Gross Profit		150,000
Dividends received		0
Less:		
Overheads (50+30)		80,000
Management charge paid/(received)		0
		80,000
Net profit		70,000
Less: dividends paid		44,000
Total retained profit		26,000
Less: minority interest share (25% of £8,000)		2,000
Retained profit belonging to group		24,000

Group Balance Sheet at 31 December 2001

	£	£
Fixed Assets (60+12)		72,000
Shares in Minor Ltd		0
Goodwill (7-3)		4,000
Current Assets		
Stock (5+3)	8,000	
Debtors	1,000	
Group debtor	0	
Cash	1,000	
	10,000	
Less:		
Creditors (8+1)	9,000	
Group creditor	0	
	9,000	
Net current assets		1,000
		77,000
Financed by:		
£1 Ordinary Shares		50,000
Retained profits		24,000
Minority interest (25% of £12,000)		3,000
		77,000

THE TREATMENT OF TAXATION

VAT

VAT-registered businesses act as tax collectors for the government. Where a company charges VAT on its sales, the VAT collected belongs to the government not the business. Therefore, sales are shown in the profit and loss account net of VAT (the same applies for expenses where VAT paid can be reclaimed).

However, for a company (or business) which cannot reclaim VAT on its inputs, the VAT paid is very much part of its costs and will be treated as such.

At the balance sheet date, there is most likely to be a VAT creditor, although some businesses (such as exporters) may be in a position where they have incurred more VAT than they have charged, ie they can reclaim more VAT than they owe to Customs and Excise. In this case, the balance sheet will show a VAT debtor.

PAYE and National Insurance

Taxes deducted from payroll are required to be paid to the authorities. These form part of the payroll expense and should be shown as such, ie included in the expenses in the profit and loss account. Likewise, the employer's National Insurance payments.

At the balance sheet date, there may be a creditor relating to moneys deducted from payroll but not yet paid over to the Inland Revenue.

Corporation tax

Companies are required to pay corporation tax on their taxable profits. This is the basis for the charge which appears in the profit and loss account.

However, the computation of corporation tax is complicated. One major difficulty is that accounting profits are not the same as taxable profits. Some expenses deducted from profit may not be tax allowable and some tax allowances may not be taken into account in calculating accounting profit, for example, capital allowances and depreciation.

To ensure that the charge for taxation appears fair in relation to the accounting profits, adjustments to the charge in the profit and loss account may be made through a deferred tax account. These adjustments attempt to reflect the different treatments of profits for tax and accounting purposes.

Final balances

There may appear several items in the balance sheet relating to corporation tax:

- Corporation tax - this is the amount of tax on the current period's profits which will have to be paid in the next accounting period.
- Deferred tax - the balance on this account represents tax to be paid on current profits at some time in the future, but not in the immediate future.

EXERCISES

1. Why do we need group accounts?

2. When is a company the subsidiary of another?

3. What are the main principles applied in producing group accounts?

4. What are the limitations of group accounts from the point of view of a third party looking to do business with a company in the group?

5. In what respects will taxation affect the financial statements of a typical commercial business?

6. Prepare the consolidated balance sheet for ABC Ltd and its subsidiary, XYZ Ltd, at 31 March 2002.

	ABC		XYZ	
Fixed assets		200,000		100,000
Investment in XYZ Ltd		100,000		
Stock	25,000		5,000	
Group debtor			15,000	
Other debtors	10,000		5,000	
Cash			4,000	
	35,000		29,000	
Less				
Creditors	8,000		1,000	
Group creditor	15,000			
Bank overdraft	10,000		3,000	
	33,000		4,000	
		2,000		25,000
Net assets		302,000		125,000
Capital				
£1 ordinary shares		200,000		100,000
Retained profits		102,000		25,000
		302,000		125,000

ABC Ltd acquired 80,000 £1 shares in XYZ Ltd for £100,000.

Effect of Solicitors' Accounts Rules 1998

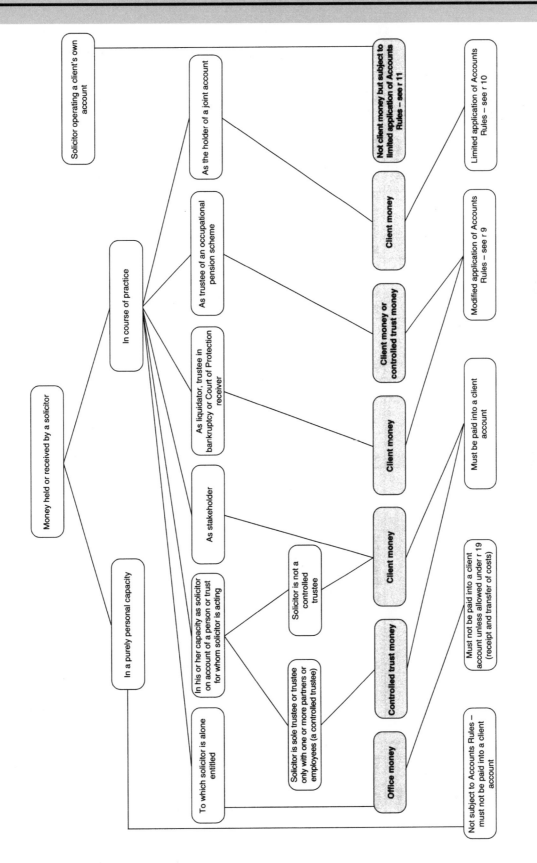

Special situations – what applies

#	Situation	Is it client money?	Subject to reconciliations?	Keep books?	Retain statements?	Subject to Accountant's Report?	Produce records to Law Society?	Interest?	Retain records generally?	Central records?	Subject to reporting accountant's comparisons?
1	Controlled trust money in client a/c – r 15(1)	No	Yes – r 32(7)	Yes – r 32(1) and (2)	Yes – r 32(9)	Yes – r 42 – same as for client money	Yes – r 34	All interest goes to trust	Yes – r 32(9)	Bills – r 32(8)	Yes – r 42(1)(f) – same as for client money
2	Controlled trust money held outside a client account – r 18	No	Yes – r 32(7)	Yes – r 32(1) and (2)	Yes – r 32(9)	Yes – r 42 – same as for client money	Yes – r 34	All interest goes to trust	Yes – r 32(9)	Bills – r 32(8)	Yes – r 42(1)(f) – same as for client money
3	Rule 16(1)(a) a/cs in solicitor's name (not client a/c)	Yes	Yes	Yes – r 32(1)(a) and (2)	Yes – r 32(9)	Yes	Yes	Yes – r 24	Yes – r 32(9)	Statements or register – r 32(11), bills – r 32(8)	Yes – r 42(1)(f)
4	Rule 16(1)(b) a/cs in name of client – not operated by solicitor	No	No	No – record solicitor's receipt and payment only	No	No	No	No – all interest earned for client – r 24, n (iii)	No – except record of solicitor's receipt and payment	Bills – r 32(8)	No
5	Rule 16(1)(b) a/cs in name of client – operated by solicitor	No	No	No – record solicitor's receipt and payment only	Yes – r 33	Limited – r 42(1)(n)	Yes – r 11	No – all interest earned for client – r 24, n (iii)	No – except record of solicitor's receipt and payment	Statements – r 32(13), Bills – r 32(8)	No
6	Liquidators, trustees in bankruptcy and Court of Protection receivers	Yes – r 9	No – r 9	Modified – statutory records – r 9	Yes – r 9 and r 32(9)(c)	Limited – r 42(1)(l)	Yes – r 9	No – r 9 – comply with statutory rules	Yes – modified r 32(9)(c)	Yes – r 32(12), Bills – r 32(8)	No – r 9
7	Trustees of occupational pension schemes	Will be either client money or controlled trust money	No – r 9	Modified – statutory records – r 9	Yes – r 9 and r 32(9)(c)	Limited – r 42(1)(l)	Yes – r 9	No – r 9 – comply with statutory rules	Yes – modified r 32(9)(c)	Yes – r 32(12), Bills – r 32(8)	No – r 9
8	Joint accounts – r 10	Yes – r 10	No – r 10	No – r 10	Yes – r 10 and r 32(9)(b)(ii)	Limited – r 42(1)(m)	Yes – r 10	No. For joint a/c with client, all interest to client (r 24, n (ix)): for joint a/c with sol. depends on agreement	No – r 10	Statements – r 32(13), Bills – r 32(8)	No – r 10
9	Solicitor acting under power of attorney	Yes	Yes	Yes	Yes	Yes	Yes	Yes	Yes	Bills – r 32(8)	Yes
10	Solicitor operates client's own a/c eg under power of attorney – r 11	No	No	No	Yes – r 33	Limited – r 42(1)(n)	Yes – r 11	No – all interest earned for client (r 24, n (iii))	No – r 11	Statements – 33, Bills – r 32(8)	No
11	Exempt solicitors under r 5	No	No	No	No	No	No	No	No	No	No

Disbursements – types of payment

NOTE: This appendix is produced for guidance purposes only. There is no substitute for analysing each type of payment by reference to the rules set out in Chaper IV of Phelps and Gizzi *VAT for Solicitors* (London: Butterworths, 2nd edn, 1993) from which this Appendix is reproduced with the kind permission of the authors.

AP = Agency Payment

GE = General Expense

DB = Disbursement

Advertising expenses	AP

Births, Marriages and Deaths – fees for searching Register of	usually GE

Commons Registration search fees	AP

Companies Registration Office fees	DB

Company search fees	usually GE

Company statutory books	AP

Completion money	DB

Costs of another party	DB
Counsel's fees	AP
Courier's fees	GE
Court fees	DB
Designs Registry search fees	usually GE
Designs Registry fees (other)	DB
Estate agents' commission	DB
Expert's fees	AP
Fax charges	GE
Foreign lawyer's fees	AP
Hotel expenses	GE
Land Registry fees	DB
Landlord's registration fees	DB
Legal database search fees	GE
Local search fees	AP
Managing agents – fees for information	AP
Mortgage redemption monies	DB

Patent search fees	usually GE
Patent Office fees (other)	DB
Patent agent's fees	AP
Photocopying charges	usually GE
Postage	GE
Sheriff's fees	AP
Solicitors instructed to act as your agents – fee of	AP
Stamp Duty	DB
Sums paid in settlement of dispute	DB
Swearing fee paid to solicitor or notary: – where affidavit/stat dec is by you	GE
– where affidavit/stat dec is by a client or a third party	AP
Telegraphic transfer fees	GE
Telephone charges	GE
Telex charges	GE
Travelling expenses	GE
Trade mark search fees	usually GE
Trade Marks Registry fees (other)	DB

Trade mark agent's fees	AP

Witnesses' expenses	DB

Wordprocessing charges	GE

Appendix 4

Further reading

Becconsall, A and Andrews, N 'Minding your Figures' Law Society's Gazette, 6 March 1996, pp 24-25.

Dencher, S 'Solicitors and VAT' Solicitors Journal, 2 June 1995, pp 528-529.

King, L 'The Solicitors' Accounts Rules: problems for fee earners' Solicitors Journal, 21 February 1997, pp 154-155.

King, L 'Solicitors' Accounts Rules 1998' Solicitors Journal, 23 October 1998, pp 968-969.

Law Society 'VAT on telegraphic transfer fees' Law Society's Gazette, 1 March 1995, p 30.

Law Society 'Accountants' Reports', Law Society's Gazette, 23 September 1992, p 16.

MacGregor, G 'The Cost of Default' Accountancy, September 1996, p 129.

MacGregor, G 'Plucking the Golden Goose's Feathers' Accountancy, June 1996, pp 98-99.

Pickering, I and Gibbens, D 'In the Dark and in the Breach' Accountancy, April 1995, pp 160-161.

Reade, A 'Solicitors' Accounts Rules 1998' New Law Journal, 5 March 1999, p 347.

Rogers, P 'Letter from the VAT man' Law Society's Gazette, 1 October 1997, p 43; 8 October 1997, p 34.

Williams, F 'On Expenses' Law Society's Gazette, 12 April 1995, p 24.

Index